Basic Computing
for the Older
Generation

Jim Gatenby

BERNARD BABANI (publishing) LTD
The Grampians
Shepherds Bush Road
London W6 7NF
England

www.babanibooks.com

Please Note

Although every care has been taken with the production of this book to ensure that all information is correct at the time of writing and that any projects, designs, modifications and/or programs, etc., contained herewith, operate in a correct and safe manner and also that any components specified are normally available in Great Britain, the Publishers and Author do not accept responsibility in any way for the failure (including fault in design) of any project, design, modification or program to work correctly or to cause damage to any equipment that it may be connected to or used in conjunction with, or in respect of any other damage or injury that may be so caused, nor do the Publishers accept responsibility in any way for the failure to obtain specified components.

Notice is also given that if equipment that is still under warranty is modified in any way or used or connected with home-built equipment then that warranty may be void.

© 2012 BERNARD BABANI (publishing) LTD

First Published – May 2012

British Library Cataloguing in Publication Data:

A catalogue record for this book is available from the British Library

ISBN 978-0-85934-731-0

Cover Design by Gregor Arthur

Printed and bound in Great Britain for Bernard Babani (publishing) Ltd

About this Book

This book is intended to help anyone who is hesitant about using computers or missed out on this new technology earlier in life. Computing as a subject is overloaded with obscure technical jargon which is off-putting to a lot of people.

This new book aims to give readers of all ages the confidence to start using computers, by explaining the basic ideas in simple terms and overcoming any fears and prejudices. Early chapters are intended to convince older people that computers are now easy to use and both young and old have much to gain in many useful, social and creative activities.

The essential components of computers and their functions are discussed so that you can make a rational choice of a machine to meet your needs. The latest Windows 7 operating system, which is both powerful and easy to use, is described in detail, including the built-in help for people with special needs.

Much has changed in recent years and this book embraces many exciting developments such as new, high performance computers, especially laptops, faster broadband Internet and wireless home networks. You can now make free Skype Internet telephone calls around the world and keep in touch with friends and family using social networking Web sites such as Facebook and Twitter.

The computer as the centre of a versatile home entertainment system for TV, music and video is also discussed.

The final chapter explains how you can use the Easy Transfer software within the Windows operating system to transfer your files from an old computer to a new one. A number of other utility programs to keep your computer, its document files and photos, etc., safe from accidental or malicious loss or damage are also described.

This book is by the same author as the best-selling and highly acclaimed "Computing for the Older Generation" (BP601).

About the Author

Jim Gatenby trained as a Chartered Mechanical Engineer and initially worked at Rolls-Royce Ltd using computers in the analysis of jet engine performance. He obtained a Master of Philosophy degree in Mathematical Education by research at Loughborough University of Technology and taught mathematics and computing in school for many years before becoming a full-time author. His most recent teaching posts included Head of Computer Studies and Information Technology Coordinator. The author has written over thirty books in the field of educational computing, including many of the titles in the highly successful Older Generation series from Bernard Babani (publishing) Ltd.

Trademarks

Microsoft, Windows, Windows XP, Windows Vista, Windows 7, Windows Live Photo Gallery, Windows Live Mail, Internet Explorer, Word, Excel, Publisher, Paint and Hotmail are either trademarks or registered trademarks of Microsoft Corporation. Norton Internet Security is a trademark of Symantec Corporation. Kaspersky Internet security is a trademark of Kaspersky Lab. BT is a registered trademark of British Telecommunications plc. All other brand and product names used in this book are recognized as trademarks or registered trademarks of their respective companies.

Acknowledgements

As usual I would like to thank my wife Jill for her continued support during the preparation of this book.

Contents

3

Types of Computer   23

4

Essential Know-how   39

5

Connecting Peripheral Devices   51

6

An Overview of Microsoft Windows 69

7

Working with Windows 81

11

Internet Activities

12

Social Networking and Communication

It's Never Been Easier

Age is No Barrier

As a former teacher of computing to students from 11 to 80 years of age and as a fully paid up member of the "Older Generation" myself, I was aware that many older people felt excluded from the new technology and lacked confidence. Many felt they would struggle to learn to use computers "at their age", especially since young children appear to have a natural talent for the subject. This impression amongst some older people is hardly surprising since children are brought up with computers in the classroom and in their bedrooms — many of us spent our schooldays poring over logarithmic tables!

To overcome this lack of confidence, I cited a friend, Arthur, who in 2002 at the age of 71 was building and repairing computers and generally acting as the neighbourhood computing expert. At the time of writing Arthur is approaching his 80th birthday and still busy solving computing problems for people a fraction of his age. Arthur does have one problem however — his own computer is often monopolised by his 92 year old mother-in-law!

Computers are cheaper and easier to use than ever before and this chapter is intended to show that there is no need for older people to miss out. Chapter 2 gives a taste of the diverse ways computers can be used to enhance your everyday life. The rest of the book explains in more detail and avoiding jargon, the skills needed to get to grips with the new technology.

In addition to helping with leisure and social activities, many of the skills covered in this book may be required when applying for a new job or starting a business.

Exploding the Myths

Despite the best efforts of publishers, adult education courses, etc., to encourage older people to start using computers, negative ideas still persist within some people. You often hear statements like "Our grandchildren are whizz kids on the computer but we haven't a clue." Some common misconceptions are as follows:

You have to be good at technical subjects like maths, physics and electronics to learn about computers.

Nonsense! Most tasks involve no more than pointing and clicking with a mouse or typing at the keyboard.

Computer software is difficult to use.

Most software uses simple ***menus*** with options or lists of choices. Alternatively you click small pictures or ***icons*** for tasks such as printing. The latest ***tablet computers*** use ***touch screens*** where you simply tap the required icon with your finger.

If you make a mistake you might damage the computer.

No need to worry. In many years of computing, I've never known anyone damage a computer by typing at the keyboard or clicking with a mouse. But computers should be moved about carefully.

You need to be a young computer "geek".

If you still think like this please read about Arthur on the previous page. Older people often have the time and patience to learn new skills and there are lots of inexpensive courses available.

The computer might lose my correspondence, accounts, family photographs, curriculum vitae or blockbuster novel.

It's true there have been cases of people losing a family photo collection or the entire text of a novel. So it's essential to make duplicate copies of valuable data, information and photos. If you use the simple backup techniques described later in this book, you need never lose a scrap of information. In producing over 30 books I don't remember losing a single page.

Modern Computers are Easier to Use

The Early Days — Learning to Program

The first "microcomputers" (as they were then known) came on the scene about 40 years ago. In those early days it really was a laborious task to make the machine achieve the most simple result. First you had to learn quite complex instructions or **program statements** and then type them in. For example, just to print the name **COMMODORE 64** on paper you had to type in the list of instructions below. (The Commodore 64 was the best-selling home computer in the 1980s.)

> **10 OPEN 4,4:CMD 4**
> **20 PRINT "COMMODORE 64"**
> **30 PRINT#4:CLOSE 4**

Computer programs have very precise rules for punctuation and syntax, etc., and are very unforgiving — even a misplaced comma or semi-colon can stop a program working. No wonder many people thought starting to use computers was too difficult!

Readymade Programs

Fortunately there were also many other people who liked writing programs and a worldwide software industry soon evolved, turning out readymade programs for every conceivable task.

New computers are now supplied with a lot of software already installed and you can also buy extra programs on CDs or DVDs and install them yourself. Nowadays most of us simply use software without writing any programs; however, every task we do on a computer uses software which has been developed by highly skilled programmers. Sometimes referred to disparagingly as "geeks", "anoraks" and "nerds", their job requires great knowledge, precision and meticulous application. Without the work of programmers the world would be a very different place — there would be no Internet, e-mail, social networking, digital photography, word processing, etc., etc., etc.

Nowadays You Just Point and Click

Readymade programs stored on the computer were a big step forward. Programs now had menus or lists of options for different tasks such as saving documents on disc or printing on paper. Initially you moved the *pointer* or *cursor* around the screen using the four arrow keys on the keyboard. When the cursor is moved over menus or icons it appears as an arrowhead, as shown on the right. At other times the cursor may be in the form of four small arrowheads or a cross-hair.

Life became even easier with the development of the WIMP *operating system* (Windows, Icons, Menus and Pointers), pioneered in America by the Xerox and Apple companies and also known as the GUI (Graphical User Interface).

The WIMP operating system used to control approximately 90% of the computers in the world is known as Microsoft Windows (or simply Windows) and it is discussed in detail throughout this book. A simple menu from Microsoft Windows is shown below.

The blue icons above are used for saving your documents on a disc. This is usually the *hard disc drive* inside the computer. The yellow icons above represent *folders* on the disc, used to store documents.

Printing a document or picture on paper is achieved by clicking the **Print** icon shown on the right and above.

The Mouse

The *mouse* is a hand-held device used to move the *cursor* around the screen and carry out tasks such as saving and printing documents. A mouse usually has at least two buttons; the left button is used to select options from a menu using a single click. For example, after typing a letter, say, you would move the cursor over the **Save** icon shown on the previous page and click the left button. **Save As** allows you to alter details such as the name with which a document is saved.

Double-clicking the left-hand mouse button is used to launch programs, such as Google, from an *icon* as shown on the right, on the **Desktop**. The Desktop is the main screen displayed after the computer has started up. Similarly you can open a Web site such as Amazon.co.uk by double-clicking a Desktop icon.

By keeping the left-hand mouse button held down you can "drag and drop" to move objects around the screen, such as pictures, photos or folders. In a similar way you can draw freehand with the mouse in a painting program or highlight a block of text for editing or formatting in a word processor.

The right-hand mouse button can be used to open "pop-up" menus with options which are relevant to objects on the screen at the current cursor position. A wheel in the centre of the mouse can be used to scroll a document up or down the screen.

Laptops use a built-in *touchpad* or *trackpad* with buttons which operate in a very similar fashion to those on a mouse. Alternatively you can easily plug a mouse into a laptop.

These topics are discussed in more detail later in this book.

The Keyboard

Despite the development of the mouse and cursor to control a computer as just discussed, the keyboard remains the normal method of entering text and numbers into a computer. Speech recognition systems are discussed later but have not so far made a significant impact on the task of text and numerical data entry. Laptop and desktop computers and some smartphones such as the Blackberry range use a QWERTY keyboard with separate physical keys. QWERTY refers to the layout of the first six letter keys. Tablet computers and smartphones such as the iPhone use the touch screen as discussed earlier.

Good keyboard skills are still a great asset for a lot of computing activities but acquiring them can take some time; most of us start off by using the one finger "hunt and peck" method to find and press the required key. After a while the skills become automatic and you start to use the fingers on both hands and hardly need to look for the keys. To speed up the learning process you might try one of the free typing tutor programs which can be downloaded from the Internet.

If you have difficulty operating a QWERTY keyboard with physical keys but you can operate a mouse, Microsoft Windows includes an On-Screen keyboard. This allows you to "type" by pointing and clicking the required letters and numbers on the image of a keyboard on the screen.

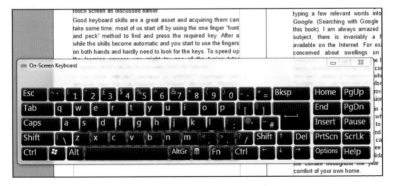

What is a Window?

The term **window** in computing refers to a rectangular area of the screen in which information or pictures are displayed. When you start up a program such as a word processor, a photo editing program or Web page, each is displayed in its own window. You can have several windows open on the screen at the same time.

Shown below is a window displaying the two previous pages from this book, open in the Microsoft Publisher program.

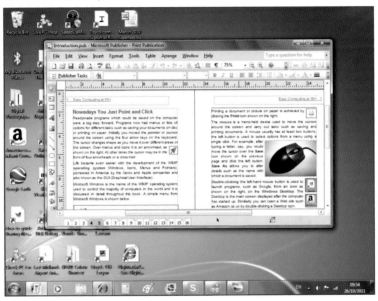

The background shown in blue on the screen above is known as the **Windows Desktop**. The small graphical images scattered about the Desktop are **icons** representing, for example, programs, Web pages or folders. Double-click an icon to open a program, Web page or folder in its own window on the screen.

A window can be enlarged or made smaller; **minimising** changes a window to appear just as a small icon on the **Taskbar** along the bottom of the screen, shown in green above.

The Microsoft Windows Operating System

Microsoft Windows is a suite of software or programs, collectively known as an *operating system* and used to manage the overall running of a computer. This is distinct from *application software*, which is used to accomplish specific tasks such as browsing the World Wide Web or writing a report, for example.

Microsoft have dominated the market for personal computer operating systems since the 1980s, first with a suite of software known as MS-DOS (Microsoft Disk Operating System). This required commands to be typed in at the keyboard.

In 1985 Microsoft's own Graphical User Interface, Microsoft Windows, was launched. The Windows operating system is currently installed on approximately 90% of the world's personal computers. At the time of writing, Windows 7 is the version currently on sale, while Windows 8 is soon to be released.

Touch Screen Technology

Windows 8 can be operated by using your fingers to touch icons on the screen, in addition to the usual mouse and cursor, as previously described. Touch screen operation allows Windows 8 to be used with *smartphones* and handheld tablet computers in addition to laptop and desktop computers. To use touch screen operation with laptop and desktop computers, you need a special touch screen monitor.

Alternative Operating Systems

The Apple Mac range of computers have been the only real alternatives to the Windows PC, (Personal Computer running the Microsoft Windows operating system). The various Mac OS operating systems have always been highly regarded for their ease of use and innovative design features.

Linux is an operating system offered for PC computers as an alternative to Microsoft Windows. Android is a popular operating system used on some smartphones and tablet computers.

Computers Can Change Your Life

Introduction

Some of the major developments in recent years which have affected the daily lives of many people are as follows:

- Powerful new laptop and tablet computers and also smartphones give easy access to computing facilities and the Internet wherever you happen to be.
- Much faster broadband Internet services make it quicker and easier to find information and download music and videos from the Internet to your computer.
- Microsoft Windows has been improved over the years making computers more powerful and easier to use.
- Web sites like Facebook and Twitter enable the worldwide exchange of news, information and photos.
- The Skype Web site provides free voice and video calls between computers around the world.
- Software which replays previously aired TV and radio.
- Inexpensive wireless *routers* enable several computers to form a home network to share resources.
- Most large companies such as Tesco and Amazon let you shop online from home while the eBay Web site helps you to sell your surplus items in an online auction.
- Many large organisations now allow form filling and financial transactions to be carried out online.
- Cheap digital cameras and personal computers enable anyone to produce high quality photographs easily.

Keeping in Touch

Electronic mail or e-mail has been around for some years, with the ability to send messages, including photographs, to friends and relatives anywhere in the world. The development of **cloud computing** using special **server** computers on the Internet for data storage now makes it easier for you to share any sort of information, including photographs, with people you trust wherever they are. The arrival of **social networking** Web sites such as **Facebook** and **Twitter** allow people to exchange instant news, messages, personal information and photographs.

Facebook allows you to search for and make contact with people you knew at school or in a previous employment, or who share similar interests. Then you can choose (or perhaps decline) to become Facebook "friends" to exchange regular news, information and photographs.

Twitter is a social networking Web site enabling you to send and read text messages or "tweets" up to 140 characters long, in order to share your latest news with friends and relatives.

Free Worldwide Video Calls

Skype is a free computer program which allows you to make voice and video calls across the Internet. Calls with Skype between computers anywhere in the world are free of charge. To download and sign up to Skype go to **www.skype.com** and left-click the **Join Skype** button on the top right of the screen. Then follow the on screen instructions. If you have friends or relatives abroad Skype can save you a great deal of money.

Making a Call

To make a call, select your contact's name from the list on the left-hand side of the Skype window. Then click **Video call** or **Call** as shown below.

Receiving a Call

When you receive a call you can answer with or without video or decline the call, as shown below.

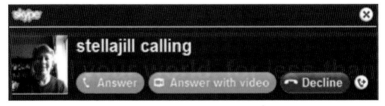

Modern laptops have the necessary built-in microphone and a *webcam* allowing you and your contacts to see each other. If necessary these accessories can also be bought separately for a few pounds; they simply plug into a laptop or desktop computer and work straightaway. As well as calls between computers, you can also use Skype to make cheap calls to mobile phones and landlines, if you have a Skype account with a credit balance.

Electronic Greeting Cards

Your computer can take care of all the greeting cards you send to friends and relatives, if they have a computer; for example, Jacquie Lawson Cards enable you to send electronic cards for every occasion — birthdays, Christmas, anniversary, etc. These *e-cards*, as they are known, consist of high quality, animated graphics with a musical accompaniment, to which you can add your own message using a pre-designed, stylish template. You receive e-mail reminders when another e-card is due, for example when a friend's birthday is approaching.

You can sign up and start sending cards at the Web site:

www.jacquielawson.com

Searching for Information on Any Subject

You can find out about virtually any subject under the sun by typing a few relevant words into a search program such as *Google*. (Searching with Google is discussed in detail later in this book). I am always amazed that no matter how bizarre a subject, there is invariably a huge amount of information available on the Internet. For example, my wife was recently concerned about swellings on the legs of our bantam chickens.

A search with Google produced a Web site with photographs which identified a condition known as "scaly mite". A further Google search for methods of treatment is shown below.

   scaly mites treatment

This quickly found numerous companies advertising sprays, etc., to treat the condition, one of which proved entirely successful.

Similarly you can find lots of information about all the illnesses which afflict the human race, provided by the NHS and other medical experts.

Many DIY tasks are explained in detail on Web sites. For example, if you need to sharpen a chainsaw or plant and stake an apple tree, you'll find lots of helpful Web pages, pictures and videos made by experts.

You can check the train or flight details for a proposed holiday, see videos of accommodation and view live *webcams* set up in holiday resorts. Then find out about the climate throughout the year, before booking online in the comfort of your own home.

Numerous Web sites provide powerful facilities for tracing your family history (as discussed later in this book) — a task previously requiring the services of a professional genealogist. Then you can place an order online for copies of birth, marriage and death certificates to be posted to you.

General Knowledge

As mentioned earlier, search programs such as Google enable you to find information on virtually any subject — Geography, History, the Arts or Science, Sport and Medicine, DIY, etc. Many of the answers are provided by Web sites such as the free online encyclopaedia **Wikipedia**. Your grandchildren might use Google to help with their homework. For example, you can find out about the great Samuel Johnson, by entering his name into Google. Numerous results appear, as shown in the extract below.

Samuel Johnson - Wikipedia, the free encyclopedia
en.wikipedia.org/wiki/Samuel_Johnson
Samuel Johnson (18 September 1709 [O.S. 7 September] – 13 December 1784), often referred to as Dr. Johnson, was an English author who made lasting ...
Life of Samuel Johnson - A Dictionary of the English Language - James Boswell

BBC - History - **Samuel Johnson**
www.bbc.co.uk/history/historic_figures/johnson_samuel.shtml
Read a biography about the life of **Samuel Johnson** who's best-known for his ' Dictionary of the English Language'.

Click each of the headings shown underlined in blue above to read the full Web pages. Online searching for information invariably produces the answers you need. Amongst many other activities, you might also use online searching for solving obscure crossword clues, for example.

Games

The Windows operating system installed on most personal computers includes a lot of games which you might enjoy, perhaps using a laptop in your favourite armchair. Some of these are card games such as Solitaire which you play alone; others, such as the strategy game Internet Backgammon, can be played online with other people around the world.

FreeCell

Getting Creative

Modern computers are now very easy to use and there is lots of affordable *software* around to enable you to accomplish virtually anything previously done by traditional methods.

Word Processing

The word processor allows you to write anything, from a short letter to a lengthy report or a book. The word processor is very forgiving, allowing you to draft and re-draft and correct mistakes to produce the perfect blockbuster you always wanted to write.

The world's leading word processor, Microsoft Word, also includes many of the features of a dedicated desktop publishing program, as discussed below.

Desktop Publishing (DTP)

Desktop Publishing software provides many additional tools to add graphic design and formatting features to a document, such as different *fonts* or styles of lettering. Large libraries of graphic images known as *clip art* are available in various categories to illustrate documents and you can also insert photographs into pages. DTP software usually includes a plentiful supply of ready-made designs for documents. These *templates* provide a professional looking format which you can customise by inserting your own text. Commonly used templates include newsletters, advertising flyers and business and greeting cards.

This book was produced using the Microsoft Publisher DTP program.

Drawing and Painting

You may wish to create a drawing of your own or modify an existing picture or photograph. Microsoft Windows includes its own easy-to-use drawing and painting program called Windows Paint. This allows you to draw freehand with a mouse and on-screen pencil tool and there is an eraser tool if you make a mistake. Alternatively you can utilise one of the ready-made shapes as shown on the right below.

Shapes can be moved around, changed in size and filled with various colours. The palette below provides a choice of colours for both lines and for infilling shapes. Click one of the black lines above the word **Size** shown below to alter the line thickness.

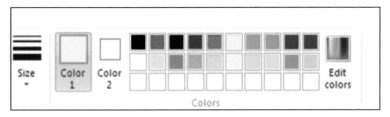

The Paint program can also be used to edit drawings and photographs. A picture can be resized or rotated in Paint. You can select and keep certain areas of a picture and discard the parts you don't want. Paint also allows you to add text to a drawing or photograph.

Digital Photography

Computers and digital cameras have transformed photography. Previously, with the traditional film camera, if you wanted to develop and print your own photographs, you needed your own dark room. Nowadays anyone with a digital camera and home computer can take photographs and make high quality prints using simple "point and click" techniques. Digital cameras have an automatic mode which takes care of complicated settings such as exposure, focusing and shutter speed, etc. A small screen on the back of a digital camera allows you to preview images straightaway and delete any you don't want.

Microsoft provides the Windows Live Photo Gallery software shown above, which can be downloaded free to your computer from the Internet. This allows you to transfer photographs from your camera and save them on your computer's hard disc drive.

Then the photographs can be edited using the Photo Gallery software as shown above. Editing can remove defects such as the "red eye" phenomenon caused by flash photography.

After editing the photographs may be printed on your inkjet or laser printer or sent to friends and family around the world using e-mail or by posting to a Web site such as Facebook or Flickr.

Music and Video

Your laptop or desktop computer can be the centre of a versatile home entertainment system. Most laptops are already equipped with sound facilities. If necessary you can also buy adequate speakers for a few pounds. This allows you to play music and videos downloaded from the Internet. Large online retailers such as Amazon and Tesco have vast libraries of music and videos to download. Then they can be saved on your computer's hard disc drive and played whenever you want. Microsoft Windows includes the Windows Media Player software shown below playing a sample video.

There are also several free media players available to download, such as iTunes and Real Player. Services such as BT Vision provide *video on demand* enabling you to pay to view TV, films and sport from their online library.

Some Web sites such as YouTube provide a lot of free videos, including popular music, mainly uploaded by individuals wanting to share with others.

Catch Up on TV and Radio

BBC iPlayer is a free service allowing you to use your computer to replay TV and radio programmes which have recently been broadcast. iPlayer can be found at:

www.bbc.co.uk/iplayer/

ITV Player, shown below, is a similar Web-based service which allows television programs to be viewed on your computer up to 30 days after first being shown on ITV. Launch ITV Player from:

www.itv.com/itvplayer/

Watch Live TV on Your Computer

You can buy a TV Tuner which plugs into your laptop or desktop computer. This turns your computer into a television, able to receive the full range of live Freeview programmes. The programmes can be watched live or saved on your computer's internal hard disc drive for viewing later. Tuner packages start around £20 and include an aerial and remote control handset.

Online News and Weather

Many local and national newspapers are available to be viewed on your computer via the Internet. National newspapers like The Times charge a small monthly fee for the online version but this is considerably cheaper than buying the newspaper every day. The online versions of many local newspapers are free. Online newspapers may be updated with the latest "breaking news", available to you as it happens, unlike the traditional paper which is usually printed the night before you read it.

Crosswords like those in The Times can be tackled online or printed out on paper. Online solutions are available the next day.

Several Internet services such as MSN and Google provide the latest news headlines, accessible at any time. Online weather forecasts from the BBC and others are immediately available for your local area or for holiday destinations at home or abroad.

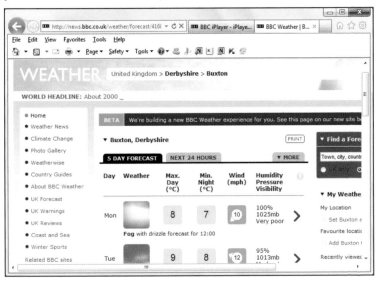

news.bbc.co.uk/weather/forecast

Watching the Pennies

It's probably more important nowadays to keep a grip on your spending than at any time in recent years. Microsoft Excel is known as a spreadsheet program, designed for handling tables of figures. It is used by large organisations around the world to produce accounts, statistics and graphs; it can equally be used to enter details of your own personal spending so that you can keep tight control of your financial affairs. The following sample spreadsheet and pie chart, based on entirely fictional data, can easily be produced using Excel on your computer without doing any arithmetic yourself, as described in detail later in this book.

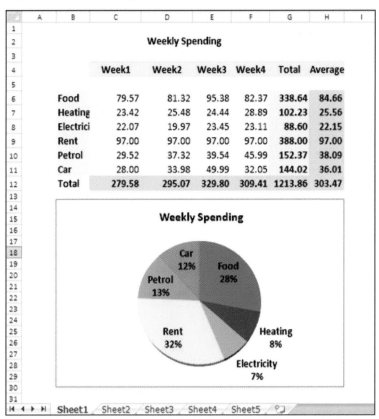

Saving Time and Money

There are many everyday tasks that can now be done *online* i.e. using a computer connected to the Internet, instead of having to travel and stand in a queue or wait days for the traditional post. Many mundane tasks can now be done more quickly from the comfort of your favourite armchair, using a laptop, at any time of the day or night. Here are just a few examples:

- Order your weekly supermarket shopping for delivery at a convenient time — saving you several hours a week.
- Raise cash by auctioning your surplus chattels on eBay.
- Complete your Income Tax Self Assessment Return.
- Tax your car by entering just a single reference number.
- Manage your bank account, check statements, set up or cancel standing orders, transfer money.
- Manage an investment portfolio — if you have one.
- Order a repeat prescription from your doctor.
- Obtain price comparisons, buy virtually anything, usually cheaper and easier than in the High Street.
- Buy or rent a house or flat, after watching an online video of the property.
- Use an online Web site to view the details and numerous photographs of second-hand cars.
- View descriptions and technical specifications of prospective purchases, e.g. electronic equipment.
- Research holidays, book flights and accommodation.
- Check in for a flight online and print a boarding pass.
- Renew your passport.
- Apply for a job, send your Curriculum Vitae by e-mail.
- Obtain a state pension forecast.
- Order copies of birth, marriage and death certificates.

Types of Computer

The Laptop Computer

The two main types of computer used in the home are the *laptop* and *desktop* machines. The laptop (also known as a *notebook*) is a complete computer system integrated into a single unit. This consists of a flat-screen monitor hinged to a slim box containing the electronic components of the computer with the keyboard on top, as shown below. The laptop computer is operated by a built-in touchpad but alternatively a mouse can be plugged in, as discussed shortly. A typical laptop has a 15 or 17 inch screen, measured diagonally. The *netbook*.is a smaller and cheaper version of the laptop with a 10 inch screen.

A Dell laptop computer

The Desktop Computer

The desktop computer normally has a separate keyboard, monitor and *base unit* (also known as a *tower*). The tower is a box containing the main working parts of the computer and usually stands on the floor, while the monitor, keyboard and mouse sit on the desk or work surface.

A desktop computer with tower unit on the floor

The flat-screen monitor, wireless mouse and keyboard shown above can be freely moved around to give the most comfortable working conditions. A large monitor is helpful when doing exacting work such as desktop publishing or computer-aided design, for example. The large monitor is also helpful if your eyesight is not what it used to be. Instead of a floor standing tower as shown above, some desktop computers have a base unit which sits flat on the desk underneath the monitor.

The All In One Desktop Computer

This is a desktop computer with a large monitor and keyboard. However, instead of having a floor standing tower or base unit containing the main electronic components of the computer, these are integrated into the monitor, together with the speakers.

Some of the latest all in one computers are operated using touch screen technology instead of a mouse. They may also have built-in devices such as webcams, card readers and microphones.

The Tablet Computer

The *tablet* is a small, light, hand held computer usually operated by a touch screen. The tablet has much of the computing capability of the laptop and desktop machines for handling e-mail, surfing the Internet, downloading music and videos, as well as games and many other applications or *apps* as they are known. The Apple iPad is the leading tablet computer but there are many others, some of which use a version of the Microsoft Windows operating system discussed throughout this book.

Samsung Tablet Computer

Some people use a tablet computer when travelling because they are so light and easy to carry. The same people also use a laptop or desktop machine for more weighty tasks at home, etc. Some tablet computers can be plugged into a *dock* which adds a physical keyboard and may include a USB port for connecting devices such as flash drives, as discussed in Chapter 5.

The Smartphone

The smartphone is a mobile phone with many computing capabilities; these include browsing the Internet, sending and receiving e-mails and downloading and playing music and videos, as well as taking digital photographs. Smartphones are usually operated by a touch screen or a small keyboard. The smartphone can easily fit into a pocket or handbag and is therefore ideal for accessing the Internet on the move. However it is not suitable for more demanding computing tasks such as desktop publishing or graphic design, for example. Two of the most popular smartphones are the Blackberry Curve and the Apple iPhone, both shown below displaying the Facebook social network Web site. The Blackberry Curve uses small physical keys while the Apple iPhone uses a touch screen keyboard.

Blackberry Curve   *Apple iPhone*

The Laptop Computer in Use

In this book, the term laptop will also include the smaller netbook computers which are basically similar but do not have a built-in CD/DVD drive.

The first laptop computers were known as "portables" and were mainly used by people doing specialist work such as travelling sales representatives and scientists working in outdoor locations. Unfortunately these forerunners of the laptop were quite heavy and not very portable so they became ironically known as "luggables". The screen display and general performance were inferior to the more traditional desktop computer and these early laptops were also very expensive.

In recent years laptops have improved by leaps and bounds and are now more than a match for desktop machines in terms of performance, screen display and price. As a result, sales of laptop machines now exceed those of desktop machines and this trend is expected to continue for the foreseeable future. While the new tablet machines are undoubtedly very popular and useful on the move, they are expected to supplement, rather than replace, the more versatile laptop machine in the next few years.

My wife Jill is not particularly interested in computers for their own sake but more as a tool for useful work, to make life easier, to save time and money and for entertainment. Jill's laptop is several years old but still going strong and used every day for diverse tasks such as checking her e-mails, supermarket shopping online, booking a holiday, managing her bank account and finding out about anything from solving obscure crossword clues to the health problems of humans, cats and poultry. One particularly useful recent task was finding a spare part for a vacuum cleaner on the Internet and ordering a replacement — the whole process only taking a few minutes. This was much easier than sending for a service engineer or visiting a shop. It's very common now for manufacturers of appliances, etc., to include instruction manuals on their Web sites.

Overheating

At one time Jill's laptop began to shut down unexpectedly, for no apparent reason. The cause of the problem was overheating. Without suitable precautions, laptops may overheat and the risk of fire can be very real. With a lot of electronic components generating heat in such a confined space, you need to make sure that the air passages are free from obstruction. Also make sure there is lots of space around the outside of the laptop and that dust doesn't build up inside the machine. Always make sure that a laptop is switched off before putting it in a bag or briefcase.

If you use a laptop literally on your lap, your clothes may block the air vents and so cause overheating. It has also been claimed that the heat from a laptop used in this manner can have adverse medical consequences, particularly for men.

Special laptop *cooling pads* are available to prevent the risk of overheating. The cooling pad consists of a small plastic tray which sits on your lap under the computer. The cooling pad has a built-in fan which is powered by the laptop through a cable plugged into one of the *USB ports* (discussed shortly).

Laptop cooling pad and fan

Alternatively use the laptop on a hard, flat surface such as a desk or table to prevent overheating when used for long periods.

Using a Laptop for Work

We also have an Inspiron laptop computer, bought online from Dell in the last year. This has quite a good specification and cost about £380. (Criteria for comparing the specification and performance of computers are discussed in Chapter 4).

The Dell Inspiron laptop is used for work such as writing this book in the evening, in the relative comfort of the house, rather than in our home office (actually a shed in the garden). I tend to use the laptop for relatively short periods of work — for longer periods of sustained effort during the day I prefer a desktop machine, as discussed shortly. For precision work I personally find it easier to use a mouse with the laptop. You can buy a plug-in mouse suitable for a laptop for under £10.

A recent newspaper article quoted a well-known physiotherapist as saying that laptops promote poor posture as you tend to look down at the screen and this can cause neck and back pain. To avoid this it was recommended that a laptop should be raised by a book or similar object so that you can see the screen without dipping your head. The report also suggested that if a laptop is used for long periods, a separate keyboard and mouse should be used, as discussed below and in Chapter 5.

The Desktop Replacement Laptop

You might need to use the same computer both on the move and as an office machine, e.g. for word processing, Desktop Publishing (DTP) and spread sheets (accounts and number crunching). You can quickly turn the laptop into an effective desktop replacement machine — simply buy and plug in a full size monitor, keyboard and mouse, as described on page 64. The connecting sockets or *ports* into which these various devices are connected are discussed in Chapter 5. Some computers are marketed as **Desktop Replacement** laptops. These are larger than the standard laptop with more powerful components, making them more expensive and not as portable.

Temporarily converting a laptop to a desktop equivalent with an extra keyboard and monitor will allow you to use the same machine both on the move and as a home office machine. This will, however, make for a rather cluttered desk As shown on page 64, compared with the normal desktop machine with just a mouse, keyboard and screen on the work surface, as shown on page 24.

As the modern laptop has built-in sound, it can also be used for listening to music and watching videos and previously shown television programmes. You can also plug in some headphones so that music or a video sound track doesn't interfere with other people in the room who may be watching television, etc. If the sound quality from your built-in speakers is not very good, this can be improved by plugging in some separate speakers costing a few pounds.

The Dell Inspiron has a built-in webcam and microphone, so that it can be used for live video calls to other people around the world using Skype (discussed earlier in this book). The webcam allows your contacts to see you as you speak and you can see them if they have a Web cam. By moving the laptop around you can also show your friends or relatives live pictures of your home, family, pets or surroundings.

The Internet

All modern laptops have a built-in adapter allowing you to connect to the Internet. This may need to be switched on before you connect to the Internet for the fist time. Connecting to the Internet is discussed in Chapter 9. Once online to the Internet, the modern laptop is ideal for the full range of Internet applications wherever you happen to be. These include tasks such as sending and receiving e-mails, communicating on Facebook and Twitter, shopping online, finding information on any conceivable subject, sending photographs around the world and downloading music and videos.

The Laptop Battery

The laptop computer relies on a battery to allow it to be used away from a mains power source. It's difficult to be precise about the time the laptop can be used before recharging is necessary because this depends on what tasks the computer is actually doing. Our elderly laptop seems to last about an hour while the newer machine seems to manage between 3 and 5 hours. Some of the latest more expensive laptops claim a fully charged battery will last up to 8 hours between charges. A warning light indicates that the battery needs recharging. Windows 7 gives an indication of the state of charge of the battery when you pass the cursor over the icon shown on the right and below on the Windows Task Bar at the bottom right of the screen.

A message also appears on the screen when the battery is running low, telling you to plug in a mains power supply. After plugging in the AC adapter, the following note appears.

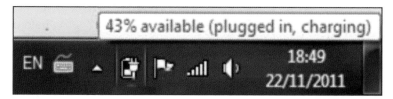

If you use battery power for long periods when you are travelling, and away from a mains power source, it's worth investing in a spare battery if you can afford it. (Laptop batteries range in price from about £20 to over £100).

The laptop package includes an AC adapter to enable the battery to be charged from a mains power point, as shown below.

Charging the battery in a laptop using an AC adapter

It is generally recommended that you run the laptop solely on battery power until the battery needs recharging, rather than keeping the AC power supply permanently connected.

Some laptops can be run on mains power alone, with the battery removed. It's usually a simple task to slide the battery out from the underside of the laptop, as shown below. However, a battery needs to be used regularly to prolong its life.

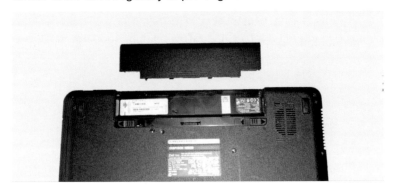

The battery slides away from the underside of the laptop

Advantages of the Laptop

- If you need to concentrate on some serious work you can use a laptop in any room in your home, away from any noise of music or television, for example.

- For less demanding tasks, you can use a laptop while relaxing in an armchair with friends or family.

- You can use your laptop at work, on the train and at home, without having to transfer documents between separate work and home computers.

- You can take a laptop and a projector to give a slide show to a club or show photographs to your friends.

- You can use a laptop when travelling and connect to the Internet using a *WIFI Hotspot* in a hotel or airport, etc.

- You can plug in a *mobile broadband dongle* and use the Internet via a mobile telephone network.

- You can print from a laptop anywhere in your home, in a bedroom, say, across a wireless network to a fixed printer in a central location such as the lounge.

- A laptop can run on either mains or battery power. So you can keep using it even if there is a power cut.

- A laptop only needs one power point for occasional use.

- A laptop doesn't take up much room in your home and can easily be stored in a cupboard when not in use. A modern laptop has built-in speakers, microphone and webcam. Also a built-in Internet connection adapter

- If necessary, for more arduous work, a laptop can easily be converted to a desktop machine by simply plugging in a full-size keyboard, monitor and mouse.

- Many new laptops have a built-in card reader for easy transfer of photographs from a digital camera.

Disadvantages of the Laptop

The laptop has many advantages for the general user, when compared with the desktop machine and some of these were summarised on the previous page. However, laptops have a few disadvantages, mainly due to their small size:

- Laptops are relatively difficult to repair since many of their components are small and "shoehorned" into a very confined space.

- Laptops are not easy to upgrade or expand by fitting newer or more powerful components.

- Laptops can be prone to overheat if care is not taken.

- The small keyboard and screen are less ergonomic than the bigger versions used on desktop computers, making the laptop less suitable for long periods of intense work.

- Laptops don't usually have a separate numeric keypad, used to facilitate the entry of large quantities of numeric data such as accounts, sales and prices, etc.

- Their small size, high value and saleability make them an attractive target for thieves.

- Laptops may get knocked about and damaged during transit if not handled with care.

- Components such as the CD/DVD drive tend to be less robust than those in the bigger desktop machines.

In spite of the above stated disadvantages, we have been using the same laptop most days for several years with no repairs required other than a wire which needed re-soldering. For the general user, the modern laptop is more than capable of carrying out the full range of computing tasks, whether for work, communication and social networking, or home entertainment.

The Desktop Computer in Use

In this section the term desktop computer usually refers to a traditional machine with a separate keyboard, monitor and tower or base unit, as shown on page 24. The main working parts of the computer are housed inside the metal or plastic casing of the tower. The tower is usually situated on the floor, leaving a clear desk for the keyboard, mouse and monitor as shown below

For many years the desktop machine was the first choice for home users, businesses and colleges, etc. While still the backbone of many organisations, sales of the desktop machine have been overtaken by the sales of laptops in recent years. This is because laptops have improved to match the desktop machine in price and performance. Another factor in the rise of the laptop is the increasing use of the Internet on trains, hotels and airports, etc., for activities like e-mail and social networking using Web sites such as Facebook and Twitter. Obviously it is not convenient to use a desktop machine while travelling.

The desktop computer needs quite a bit of space in your home – perhaps a special computer desk set up in a corner of your lounge, or in a spare bedroom if you have one. When setting up a home office, many people, including myself, use a shed in the garden. The desktop machine needs several power points for the separate tower unit, monitor and speakers. Despite the above drawbacks, many people including myself, continue to favour the desktop machine for some applications in certain situations.

My main desktop machine is of indeterminate age. This is because you can replace the main parts easily and mine has had several replacement monitors, keyboards and major internal components over the years. This is cheaper than buying a complete new machine to keep up with the latest developments in software, which continually require more powerful computers.

I recently fitted an extra large monitor (24 inches measured diagonally) shown on page 35, to improve readability. A new full size replacement keyboard was bought for under £10.

In the tower unit of a desktop computer, the critical electronic components needed to control facilities such as the graphics displayed on the screen or the sound quality, are stored on small removable circuit boards called *expansion cards*. Each of these is usually held in place by a single screw. An expansion card which controls the screen graphics is shown below.

An expansion card used to control graphics

A graphic designer, writer, photographer or games player, for example, might want to improve the graphics capability of their machine. They could simply buy and fit a better (and more expensive) graphics card. Similarly a person interested in music could improve the sound quality by fitting a better **sound card** (also known as an **audio card**). Such improvements are simple to carry out on the desktop computer but very difficult, if not impossible, with the laptop.

The desktop computer tower unit is very easy to assemble and many people, including myself, have built their own computers from kits — it's really just a case of screwing the parts together and connecting the cables. This can save a lot of money and at the same time you learn a lot about the computer — it's no longer just a complicated magic box that can perform miracles.

Unlike modern laptops, the traditional desktop computer doesn't normally have built-in devices like a webcam, speakers, card reader, or microphone, although these items can each be bought separately for a few pounds. You simply plug them into one of the sockets or **ports** on the tower unit (discussed in Chapter 5). They usually work straightaway or very soon after a short, automatic installation process. Some monitors have built-in speakers and you can also buy plug-in head phones, which may incorporate a microphone. These peripheral devices are discussed in more detail in Chapter 5.

A plug-in webcam which also has a built-in microphone

Advantages of the Desktop Computer

- Desktop machines generally have larger, separate screens and keyboards, making them easier and less tiring to use for demanding work over long periods.

- The tower unit situated on the floor provides a less cluttered desk or work surface.

- Components are easily replaced in the desktop machine, making repairs and upgrades simpler and cheaper.

- Components in desktops have more space and air around them, reducing the risk of overheating.

Disadvantages of the Desktop Computer

- The desktop machine takes up more space than a laptop and needs to be permanently set up in a fixed location.

- The desktop machine can't be used on the move on trains and in airports and hotels, for example.

- The desktop machine needs several power points for the monitor, tower unit and speakers, etc.

- The desktop computer can't be used during a power cut.

- Peripheral accessories such as speakers, microphones, webcams and card readers are not usually built into desktop computers and need to be bought separately.

- It's relatively complicated transferring a document between two desktop computers in different places.

Summary: Laptop or Desktop or Both?

Either a laptop or a desktop machine will satisfy most of your general computing needs. If you need both a laptop for computing on the move and an office based desktop machine, buying two new machines may be too expensive. So you might consider buying a second-hand machine. These can be obtained for under £100 on eBay or in your local newspaper.

Essential Know-how

Introduction

Earlier chapters of this book attempted to show that older people can enjoy using computers and benefit from their many diverse and worthwhile applications. Chapter 3 argued the pros and cons of various types of computer and concluded that both laptop and desktop machines are eminently suitable for most older people. Tablet computers and smartphones are useful and entertaining for people on the move, but as a supplement rather than a complete replacement for the laptop or desktop machine.

The vast majority of laptop and desktop computers in the world (and some tablet computers and smartphones) are managed and controlled by the Microsoft Windows operating system. The current version, Windows 7, is referred to throughout this book and most of the material also applies to Windows Vista and XP.

Computing, being a relatively new technology, is riddled with its own specialist jargon, not surprisingly creating a language which many people find confusing. This chapter describes the essential components common to all computers and attempts to use plain English to demystify the jargon surrounding them. If you understand the basic principles underlying the operation of all personal computers, you will be able to:

- Choose a computer with a specification which meets your own present and future needs.

- Avoid being blinded with science by unscrupulous people trying to sell computers, equipment or software.

- Use your computer more effectively and understand the need for sound backup and security procedures.

What is a Computer?

One definition of a computer is a machine which can carry out a *program* or sequence of stored instructions. The program consists of a list of statements, usually in a *programming language* based on English but with a syntax or grammar of its own. A very simple example of part of a program is shown on page 3. The program statements are instructions which tell the computer what to do, such as printing a word, making a sound or drawing a line, etc.

Where are programs permanently stored?

So that programs are always available to be *executed* or "run", they are permanently stored or recorded on a magnetic disc. This is usually the *hard disc drive*, as shown below, which revolves at high speed inside the case of the computer.

A hard disc drive with its top casing removed

When you buy a new computer, some programs will already have been installed i.e. saved on the hard disc drive. You can buy additional programs on a CD or DVD and copy them to your hard disc drive. Nowadays many programs can also be *downloaded* from the Internet over the telephone lines and saved on your hard disc drive.

Apart from programs, the hard disc can also hold *data files*, i.e. the words and numbers you are working with such as a list of names and addresses, photos, videos or the text of a document.

What is the memory?

In order to run or execute a program, it is copied or "loaded" into a temporary storage area known as the *memory*. The memory consists of one or more *modules* each containing a number of chips mounted on a small circuit board, as shown below.

A memory module or DIMM

The memory only holds the programs you are currently running at a given point in time, unlike the hard disc drive which contains your entire collection of programs.

The memory also holds the data files such as documents you may be working on using the current program.

When the computer is switched off the contents of the memory are completely wiped. This sort of memory is said to be *volatile* and is known as *RAM* or *Random Access Memory*.

How are programs run or executed?

In order to carry out the instructions in a program they are fetched from the memory and executed in the *processor*, also known as the *microprocessor*, *CPU* or *Central Processing Unit*, as shown on the right. The processor is a single chip, often called the "brains" of the computer, since it carries out calculations and logical operations.

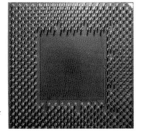

An AMD Athlon processor

After an instruction has been executed, the result of the operation is transferred back to the memory and may be displayed on the screen.

Saving a Document

If you are working on a document such as a report, for example, the data consists of the letters you type in using the keyboard. This data will be held in the memory or RAM until you overwrite it with new data or switch the machine off. In either case the document will be lost. So to keep a permanent copy of a document you must carry out a *save* operation to record it permanently on your hard disc drive or other storage medium such as a *flash drive* or CD/DVD.

Volatile versus "Permanent" Memory

Programs and data stored in the memory, i.e. RAM, are lost when the computer is switched off. The memory is said to be *volatile*.

The hard disc drive, flash drive and rewriteable CD or DVD are a type of permanent or *non-volatile* storage. Programs and data stored on these media are not lost when the computer is switched off. The word permanent is used loosely here, because you can, if you wish, remove programs and data from a hard disc drive, flash drive or rewriteable CD or DVD (designated CD-RW and DVD-RW). All of these rewriteable media can be repeatedly used for saving data, which can, if necessary, be deleted or overwritten. CD-R and DVD-R can only be written to once and cannot be overwritten with new data.

Flash Memory

This is a type of non-volatile memory which can be used to save data. The data is not lost when the computer is switched off. It can also be wiped and re-used like the hard disc drive. Flash memory is used in flash drives, also known as memory sticks, and camera memory cards. The iPad tablet computer uses flash memory instead of a hard disc drive as non-volatile memory.

Computer Performance Criteria

The previous pages described some of the main components involved in the computing process, namely:

- The hard disc drive used for permanently storing programs and data.

- The memory or RAM which holds temporarily the instructions and data for the current programs.

- The processor or CPU used for carrying out instructions such as calculations and other logical operations.

The above components are critical to the performance of a computer and are often the main criteria used to compare and sell computers. Obviously the larger the hard disc, the more programs and data can be stored before you need to start deleting *files*. If a computer has insufficient memory or RAM for the program or data being executed, the computer will run very slowly. Similarly a slow processor may be unable to handle complex calculations or fast moving graphics in a game.

The following is part of a typical specification used to advertise laptop and desktop computers:

> ## ACE Laptop Computer
>
> - **Intel Core Duo 2.6GHz**
> - **4GB Memory**
> - **320GB Hard Drive**
>
> **£399 including VAT**

The above jargon is explained on the next few pages.

Jargon Explained

Intel Core Duo 2.6GHz

This note on the previous page refers to the processor or CPU as discussed earlier. *Intel* is the name of the manufacturer and *Core Duo* is the type of processor. *2.6GHz* is a measure of the speed of the processor to carry out instructions such as arithmetic, for example. The processor incorporates a *clock* which generates electronic pulses or cycles. This determines the speed the computer can carry out instructions.

1GHz is a measure of frequency and means 1,000,000,000 cycles per second.

I often use a 1.60GHz Windows 7 computer for general tasks such as typesetting books like this one, creating spreadsheets (financial calculations) and surfing the Internet. The performance of a 1.60GHz processor is quite adequate for this type of work. However, for certain applications, such as complex graphics, multimedia work and the latest games, a more powerful processor may be required. Processor speeds ranging from 2 to 3GHz are typical on new computers at the time of writing.

Microsoft recommend a processor speed of 1GHz or faster to run the Windows 7 operating system.

4GB Memory

When notes like this appear in advertisements it is referring to the size of the memory or RAM measured in Gigabytes (GB), as explained on the next page. Memory or RAM is introduced on page 41 and is used to store the instructions and data for the programs currently being run or executed.

At the current time, new computers costing around £300-£400 have a typical memory of 3 or 4GB while more expensive machines have 6 or 8GB. We run the Windows 7 operating system successfully on machines with 2GB of RAM and Microsoft recommend at least 1GB or preferably 2GB, depending on the specification of the processor. (Please see page 46).

Adding Extra Memory

If a computer doesn't have enough memory, a program will run slowly. Increasing the size of the memory is one of the simplest and cheapest ways to increase the performance of a laptop or desktop computer. You simply add extra memory modules or replace existing modules with new ones of higher capacity. All you need is a screw driver to remove the computer's casing and the memory modules just clip into place.

Bits and Bytes — Units of Memory Size

Inside the computer, data and instructions are converted to the *binary code*, where everything is represented electronically by strings of 0s and 1s. So, for example, the letter A might be coded as 1000001. The 0s and 1s are known as *binary digits* or *bits* for short. Every letter of the alphabet, number, punctuation mark, keyboard character or program instruction can be represented by groups of bits. These are usually arranged in groups of 8 bits each known as a *byte*. As computers have become more powerful over the years, memory or RAM sizes have been quoted first in *kilobytes*, then in *megabytes* and nowadays in *gigabytes,* as defined below.

Byte	A group of 8 binary digits (0s and 1s) or bits. A byte may be used to represent a digit 0-9, a letter, punctuation mark or keyboard character, for example.
Kilobyte (K):	1024 bytes
Megabyte (MB):	About 1 million bytes (1,048,576 to be exact).
Gigabyte (GB):	About 1 billion bytes (1,073,741,824 to be exact).

*When buying a new computer, choose one with as much **RAM** and as fast a **processor** as you can afford.*

320GB Hard Drive

This was the final part of the computer specification shown at the bottom of page 43. The hard disc drive, as shown on page 40, is like a filing cabinet containing all your programs and data files. The terms *hard drive*, *hard disc* and *hard disk* are all terms used to refer to the *hard disc drive*. (*Disk* is the American spelling). An early form of magnetic data storage was a flimsy magnetic disc called the *floppy disc*, which is now obsolete. The hard disc drive is so called because it is not floppy but instead uses rigid metal discs or *platters*. *320GB* above refers to the amount of space on the hard disc drive available to store programs and data. As a rough guide, and referring to the definitions at the bottom of page 45, a book such as this one stored on the hard disc drive would take up about 50MB (megabytes) or a twentieth of a gigabyte of hard disc space.

As well as data files such as text and photographs, etc., the hard disc drive also contains all of the programs, including all of the files which make up the Windows operating system. Microsoft recommend at least 16GB or 20GB of free hard disc space to accommodate Windows 7, depending on which version of Windows 7 you are using. There are two types of *computer architecture* known as *32-bit* and *64-bit* — these refer to the size of the "chunks" of data that the processor and the various *data buses* or *highways* inside the computer can handle and move around. There are separate versions of Windows 7 for computers using 32-bit and 64-bit architecture.

A relatively inexpensive computer costing around £300 would have a typical hard disc drive capacity of around 300GB.

More expensive machines (both laptop and desktop) costing around £1000 or more might have a hard disc capacity of 1 or even 2TB (Terabytes).

1 Terabyte (TB) = 1,000GB =1,000,000,000,000 bytes

Checking the Specification of a Computer

If you want to know what processor, memory and hard disc drive a computer contains, this can be checked using the Windows operating system.

Click the **Start** button in the bottom left-hand corner of the screen, as shown on the right. Then click the word **Computer** from the right-hand panel of the **Start** menu, shown on the right.

The **Computer** window opens as shown below.

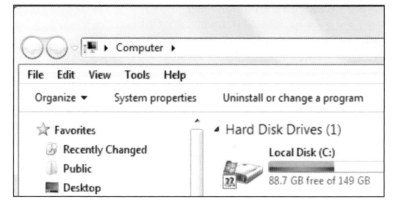

From the window above you can see that this particular computer has a hard disc drive called **Local Disk (C:)** with a nominal capacity of **149GB** of which **88.7GB** are free.

Now click **System properties**, as shown in the centre above, and the **System** window appears, as shown in the extract below.

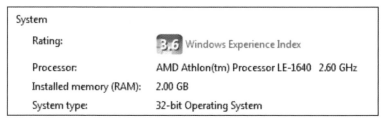

Referring to the screen shot at the bottom of the previous page, you can see that this desktop computer has an **AMD Athlon** processor running at **2.6GHz**. The screenshot also shows that the computer has **2.0GB** of installed memory or RAM as discussed on page 44 and 45. This screen shot refers to my main desktop computer which was built from a kit a few years ago. It happily runs Windows 7 and has been used for much of the work on this book.

The Specification of a Windows 7 Laptop

The specification of our Dell laptop was checked as described on the previous page and the results are shown on the right and below.

You can see from the above details that the Dell laptop has twice as much memory and a bigger capacity hard disc than the desktop machine listed on the previous page. Processor speed is similar in both cases but the laptop has a **64-bit Operating System,** compared with the 32-bit system on the desktop machine. 64-bit and 32-bit refer to the size of the chunks of data which can be handled by the computer. A computer with a 64-bit processor and 64-bit *data highways* inside the computer can get through more work than a 32-bit system.

3.4 Windows Experience Index shown above is a measure of the computer's overall performance in the range 1.0 to 7.9. A rating above 3.0 is required to run Windows 7.

The Specification of a Windows XP Computer

To display the specification of a computer running Windows XP, click the **Start** button at the bottom of the screen, as shown on the right. Then select **My Computer** 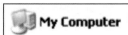 from the Windows XP Start Menu. As shown in the extract from the **My Computer** window below, details of the hard disc drive are displayed in the left-hand panel.

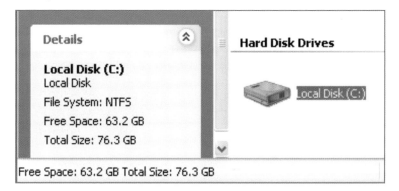

The left-hand side of the **My Computer** window also displays the menu shown on the right. Now click **View system information** and the details of the computer's processor and RAM are displayed, as shown on the right below.

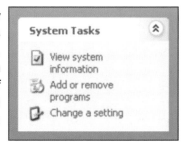

You can see that this desktop computer, which happily runs Windows XP, has only 448MB or less than half a gigabyte of memory or RAM. This compares with 4GB in the Dell laptop.

Summary: The Critical Components

This chapter has described three critical components which affect the performance of a computer. These are the processor or CPU, the memory or RAM and the hard disc drive. These components are a major part of the sales specification of new computers and familiarity with them is essential when buying or using computers.

Over time the specification of these components increases as computers are developed to utilise new software such as Windows 7 or 8, for example. This is borne out by the specification of my nearly new Dell laptop and my older and inferior Windows XP desktop machine, shown on the previous two pages. The *minimum* hardware requirements recommended by Microsoft for Windows XP and Windows 7 are shown below.

Operating System	Processor Speed	Memory RAM	Hard Disc Space
Windows XP	300MHz	128MB	1.5GB
Windows 7 32-bit	1GHz	1GB	16GB
Windows 7 64-bit	1GHz	2GB	20GB

(Please see page 45 and 46 for definitions of the above units).

As shown above, the hardware requirements for the two current Windows 7 operating systems are much greater than those for the earlier Windows XP operating system. Therefore, to keep up to date with the latest software developments, you need to buy a computer with the highest specification that you can afford.

As discussed earlier in this chapter, the RAM can easily be upgraded on both laptop and desktop computers, even by the ordinary user with no special skills. Changing the processor and hard disc drive are more difficult tasks, especially on laptops. If you don't feel able to tackle this work, there are plenty of small local computer repair businesses who can carry out such upgrades, in order to prolong the life of a cherished computer.

Connecting Peripheral Devices

Introduction

The previous chapter discussed three essential components at the heart of the computer, namely the processor, the hard disc drive and the memory. In order to make a computer useful and versatile, you need to be able to connect various peripheral devices which can be used for the *input* and *output* of data.

Input

Input data might, for example, include photographs to be transferred from the memory card inside your camera. Or a document you've been working on using a different computer and saved on a removable flash drive or memory stick. Or you might want to copy some music from a CD or DVD. You can also input data in the form of text, pictures and also software by *downloading* from the Internet. The data you input to your computer would normally be saved on the hard disc drive.

Output

Data output would include displaying words and pictures on the monitor or screen, using a printer to make a "hard copy" on paper, or using speakers or headphones to output music or the sound track for a video, etc. Data such as text and photographs can be output from your computer and *uploaded* to a Web site.

The CD/DVD drive is a peripheral device used for both the input and output of data. It is normally built in as an integral part of a laptop or desktop computer. You can also buy external CD/DVD drives and hard disc drives with cables which plug into laptop and desktop computers, as discussed later.

The Input and Output Ports

In order to connect the peripheral devices to laptop and desktop machines, a number of sockets, known as *ports*, are provided on the outside of most computers. The ports are normally along the sides of a laptop computer and on the back of a desktop machine. Using these sockets you can connect a wide range of useful devices. Then data can be input to the memory before being transferred to the CPU for processing, before the results are output to the monitor or printed on paper, for example.

The VGA (Video Graphics Array) Port

This is the standard 15-pin port, used on desktop and laptop computers to connect a monitor. Laptop computers, as well as having an integral monitor, normally have a VGA port to enable a separate monitor to be

VGA port

connected, if required. The VGA port can also be used to connect a projector, e.g. for giving a talk or slide show.

The DVI (Digital Video Interface) Port

Some computers have a *DVI* port which gives a superior quality screen display on a suitable monitor. The monitor must have a DVI socket to accommodate the special cable from the DVI port on the computer. On desktop computers it's easy to fit a new DVI graphics card to replace a standard VGA graphics card. Some expensive laptop computers are fitted with a DVI port as standard. Shown below is a graphics card containing both a blue VGA graphics port and a white DVI graphics port. The graphics card in a desktop computer is simply pushed into a slot in the *motherboard* and is held in place by a single screw.

VGA graphics port   *DVI graphics port*

The Ethernet Port

Although many homes now use wireless networks, businesses often prefer cabled or wired networks. These are acknowledged to be faster than wireless networks but do require holes to be drilled in walls and cabling installed throughout the building.

Ethernet port

Most wired networks use a technology known as *Ethernet*; this refers to the cables, built-in network adapters and Ethernet ports, as shown on the right. An Ethernet port and network adapter are fitted as standard on laptop computers and on many desktop computers. If not, it's a simple and inexpensive task to fit a network card to a desktop computer. Even on a wireless network it's often necessary to use an Ethernet cable between the *router* and the computer during the initial setting up process.

Many hotels have a wired Ethernet network with sockets in the bedrooms, allowing guests to connect to the Internet. All you need is a laptop computer and a short Ethernet cable.

The Audio or Sound Ports

Laptop Computer

Laptops normally have a built in microphone and sound facilities. In addition there are usually two input and output ports to connect a separate microphone and speakers. These ports are usually inconspicuous, small, round apertures in the laptop casing.

Desktop Computer

The ports shown on the right are used to connect audio devices to a desktop computer. The green port is used for sound output to speakers or headphones, pink is for input from a microphone while light blue is used for audio input, such as from an external CD drive. You might want to fit a better sound *expansion card* to improve the quality of the sound. Fitting a better sound card is a job anyone can accomplish.

Audio ports

PS/2 Ports

These are still commonly used on desktop computers to connect the cables for a separate keyboard and a mouse. The green PS/2 port shown on the right is used to connect the mouse cable while the purple PS/2 port is used for the keyboard connection.

PS/2 ports

The laptop computer, with its built-in keyboard and touch pad doesn't need PS/2 ports as shown above. Nowadays many people prefer to use a *wireless* mouse and keyboard, thus reducing the clutter on the desk or work surface. You can also buy keyboards and mice which plug into the *USB* ports discussed below. If you want to use a full size keyboard and a mouse on a laptop, both wireless and USB devices are available.

USB (Universal Serial Bus) Ports

A few years ago, most personal computers had a variety of different ports to connect specific devices.

These include the *parallel* or *Centronics* port for connecting a printer, and the *serial* or *COM* port for connecting a mouse or *modem*. Nowadays these ports have largely been replaced by USB ports, although they are still present on some desktop computers.

USB port

USB ports are a relatively new development but they are taking over as the standard method for connecting virtually any sort of peripheral device. The USB ports are small rectangular slots; on a desktop computer there are usually four USB ports at the back of the base unit and sometimes a further two at the front. Laptops usually have three or four USB ports on the side of the computer. USB technology has developed over recent years to give increasing speeds for data transfer between computers and peripheral devices. More expensive computers may have a mixture of USB 2.0 and USB 3.0 ports. USB 2.0 is still in widespread use while USB 3.0 is the latest high speed standard.

The USB port has many advantages over the earlier *serial* and *parallel ports*, which were bulky and expensive:

- USB devices, such as a digital camera, can be plugged in or removed while the computer is up and running. You should, however, wait until the computer has finished saving data before removing a device like a flash drive, as discussed shortly.

- USB connections are simple, cheap and light and easy to plug in and remove.

- Some USB devices are known as *plug and play*, because they work as soon as they are plugged in for the first time. These plug and play devices don't need special installation software, known as *device drivers,* supplied on a CD/DVD by the manufacturers of some devices.

- The USB specification in general use over the last few years is USB 2.0, while the latest standard, USB 3.0 is becoming increasingly available in new devices such as flash drives. USB 3.0 is also known as SuperSpeed as it gives data transfer rates many times faster than USB 2.0 devices. Some new laptop computers are supplied with a mixture of some USB 2.0 ports and a USB 3.0 port for high speed devices. These include applications where large amounts of data need to be transferred between the device and the computer, such as flash drives, external hard disc drives, digital cameras, camcorders and CD/DVD and Blue Ray external drives.

- USB 3.0 devices are designed so that they can still work with computers designed for the older USB 2.0 standard. Similarly computers built to the new USB 3.0 standard can still run devices designed for the older USB 2.0 standard. Obviously to get the maximum benefit of the high speed technology both the device and the computer ports need to be of the USB 3.0 design.

USB Dongles

As just described, the USB ports can be used for connecting a diverse range of devices. Some of these devices, such as printers, are connected to a USB port on the computer using a USB cable. However, many other small USB devices plug directly into a USB port and are collectively known as *dongles*. A typical dongle may only be the size of a little finger but can contain the electronics to carry out some very complex functions. Shown below are several dongles for various purposes.

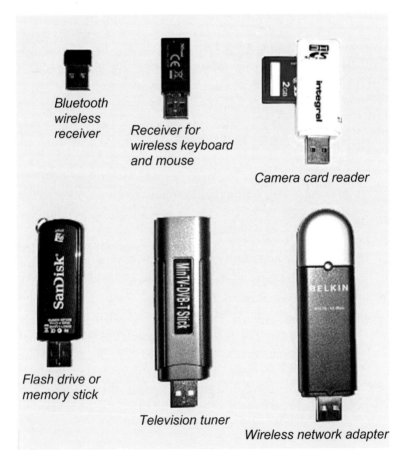

Bluetooth wireless receiver

Receiver for wireless keyboard and mouse

Camera card reader

Flash drive or memory stick

Television tuner

Wireless network adapter

The USB Flash Drive (Memory Stick)

This is a very popular type of USB dongle. It's used for saving data files such as text, music and photographs. I find flash drives particularly useful for transferring files between computers in different places, such as work and home. The flash drive can also be used to make *backup* copies of files saved on the hard disc drive.

Flash drive or memory stick

Unlike the computer's main memory or RAM, the data on the flash drive is non-volatile — you don't lose it when the power to the computer is switched off or the dongle is removed. The flash drive behaves more like the computer's internal hard disc drive. Like the hard disc drive, the flash drive is a read/write device — allowing files to be saved or deleted repeatedly. This includes overwriting an earlier document by a later one with the same name. Unlike the hard disc drive, which rotates at high speed, the flash drive contains no moving parts and is a form of *solid state* memory, similar to the memory cards used in digital cameras and used as the main memory in tablet computers.

Some dongles can be *write protected* by moving a small switch as shown in red on the SanDisk flash drive above. In the closed position no data can be written to or deleted from the flash drive.

At the time of writing an 8GB USB 2.0 flash drive can be obtained for under £5.00, while a 32GB drive costs around £25. (Please see page 45 for definitions of units of memory size such as GB). USB 3.0 flash drives are also available but a little more expensive. As discussed earlier, you will only get the increased speed of data transfer from a USB 3.0 flash drive if your computer supports the USB 3.0 standard. Methods of upgrading laptop and desktop computers from USB 2.0 to USB 3.0 are discussed on page 59.

Devices Connected via USB Ports

- A *dongle* for a wireless keyboard and mouse, giving a less cluttered desk and freedom of movement.

- A USB *broadband modem* to connect a single computer to the Internet via the telephone lines.

- A USB *wireless (WiFi) adapter* to connect a desktop computer to the Internet via a *wireless router*. (WiFi adapter built in as standard on a new laptop computer).

- A USB adapter to connect a *Bluetooth* device such as a mobile phone to a computer to transfer data wirelessly.

- An USB inkjet or laser printer used to print text, pictures or photographs.

- An external hard disc drive giving additional storage and enabling the backup of the internal hard drive.

- USB flash drive, also known as a memory stick, used to back up data files and transfer files between computers.

- USB headphones, webcam, speakers and microphone for improved sound or use free video calls on Skype.

- A digital camera or camera phone connected via a USB cable, enabling photos to be transferred to a computer.

- A *card reader* to transfer photographs from a memory card removed from a digital camera. Laptops often have a built-in card reader.

- A *mobile broadband dongle*, used to connect a laptop to the Internet wherever a signal can be obtained using a mobile telephone network.

- A *TV Tuner dongle* enabling you to receive live television on a laptop or desktop computer.

- An external CD/DVD or the latest *Blue Ray* drive.

- A flatbed scanner for inputting paper documents.

Adding USB Ports

USB ports are now used for so many peripheral devices that you may need to add some extra ones in addition to the 3-6 ports already provided on a new laptop or desktop computer.

If you just want to increase the number of ports on a laptop or desktop computer for example, a simple way is to buy a *USB hub* such as the one shown on the right. This cost a few pounds and converts one USB port into four.

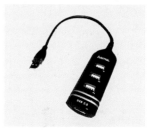

4-port USB hub

In a desktop computer you can also add extra ports by fitting a USB expansion card. As discussed earlier, you simply remove a few screws and take off the computer's casing. The USB expansion card plugs into a slot in the *motherboard*, the large circuit board inside the computer's casing. The expansion card is held in place by a single screw. Shown on the right is an expansion card providing four extra USB ports.

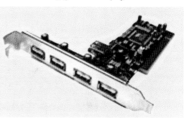

4-port USB expansion card

Upgrading from USB 2.0 to USB 3.0

A desktop computer can be converted from USB 2.0 to USB 3.0 by fitting a PCI Express USB 3.0 expansion card, similar to the one shown above. Laptops having a built-in *ExpressCard* slot can be fitted with a USB 3.0 ExpressCard as shown on the right.

2-port USB 3 ExpressCard

Using a USB Flash Drive

You can insert a flash drive (or any other USB device) into any of the USB ports in your computer. If the computer has a mixture of USB 2.0 and USB 3.0 ports, you would obviously use the USB 3.0 port if high speed data transmission was needed for transferring very large files, such as videos, etc.

When you install a flash drive into a computer for the first time, it is automatically detected. The Windows operating system then looks for and installs the necessary *device driver* software to make the device work with your computer, as shown below.

After a very short time, the software installation process is complete and, all being well, the following note appears in the bottom right-hand corner of the screen.

Installing the device driver software is a one-off operation, only needed the first time you insert the flash drive into a particular computer. If you remove the flash drive and insert it in a different computer for the first time, the one-off driver installation process will need to be done on that computer.

In future, whenever you plug the flash drive into a USB port in a computer in which it has been previously inserted, the **AutoPlay** window should appear, as shown on the next page.

If the **AutoPlay** window doesn't open as described on the next page, follow the notes on page 62 to open the **AutoPlay** window using the Windows Explorer.

Viewing a Flash Drive Using AutoPlay

The AutoPlay window opens soon after a flash drive is inserted into a USB port, as shown below. This menu contains various options depending on the sort of files stored on the flash drive. If the flash drive contains photos, there are options to import them into you computer and save them on the hard disc drive.

If you click **Open folder to view files**, the **Computer** window displays the files saved on the flash drive, as shown below. **BP601 Colour** highlighted in blue is a folder containing chapters of this book. The other files are software provided by the makers of the flash drive, in this example a **Kingston Data Traveller**.

If the AutoPlay Menu Doesn't Open

If the AutoPlay menu doesn't appear as shown on page 61, click the Windows Explorer icon shown on the right, found on the Taskbar at the bottom left of
the screen. Then right-click the name or icon for the memory card in the Windows Explorer. It may be labelled **Removable Disk (E:) or (F:)**, etc. From the menu which appears click **Open AutoPlay...** as shown on the right.

Expand

Open as Portable Device

Open AutoPlay...

Viewing a Flash Drive in the Computer Window

When a flash drive has been inserted into a USB port and detected by the Windows operating system, it can then be used like the hard disc drive, as a medium for saving and deleting files. To view the flash drive, click the **Start** button at the bottom left corner of the screen and then click **Computer** from the Start Menu. The **Computer** window opens as shown below.

▲ Hard Disk Drives (1)

Local Disk (C:)

88.9 GB free of 149 GB

▲ Devices with Removable Storage (3)

Floppy Disk Drive (A:)   DVD RW Drive (D:)   KINGSTON urDrive (E:)

1.82 GB free of 7.45 GB

When you insert a flash drive into a USB port it is assigned a name such as **Removable Disk (E:) or (F:)**. As shown above, the flash drive in this particular example appears as **Kingston urDrive (E:)**. **Floppy Disk Drive (A:)** shown above represents a type of data storage which is now virtually obsolete, having been replaced by the far superior flash drive. Double click the flash drive icon such as **KINGSTON** shown above to view the files on the drive, as shown at the bottom of page 61.

Removing a Flash Drive (or another USB Device)

When using a flash drive to save a document or photo, etc., always wait until the saving process is complete before removing the flash drive — otherwise some of your data may be lost.

Windows provides a green icon with a tick which tells you when it's safe to remove hardware from a USB port. This icon appears on the Taskbar at the bottom right of the screen, as shown on the right and below.

 If the green icon doesn't appear on your Taskbar, click the **Show hidden icons** icon shown here on the left and on the Taskbar above. The small window shown on the right appears and this should include the green icon.

Pass the cursor over the green icon, which then displays the words **Safely Remove Hardware and Eject Media**. Now click the green icon and then click **Eject** next to the required device on the pop-up menu, as shown below. In this example, the device to be removed is the Kingston Data Traveller flash drive, **DT 101 G2**.

The message below appears and you can now safely remove the device, in this example a flash drive, from the USB port.

Using a Laptop as a Desktop Computer

The USB ports and the VGA port on a laptop computer can be used to attach a separate monitor and a full-size keyboard and mouse. (On this page the term laptop also refers to the smaller netbook machines). This might be helpful, for example, if you are doing a lot of word processing or data entry or your eyesight is not as good as it used to be. A 19-inch TFT slimline monitor can be bought for under £100 and connects to the VGA port on the laptop. A full-size USB keyboard and mouse can be added for about £15 or less. These plug into the USB ports on the laptop and are immediately detected and soon ready for use. As shown below, the small laptop or netbook computer can now be used with all the ergonomic advantages of a desktop machine.

Connecting a laptop computer to a separate monitor, keyboard and mouse using USB cables and a VGA monitor cable.

Alternatively you can plug a *USB mini receiver* into a USB port on the laptop to connect a *wireless* mouse and keyboard.

Types of Printer

A printer is essential for many applications of the personal computer, whether you're printing holiday photographs, preparing a newsletter, producing flyers to advertise a local event, or writing a book, such as this one, for example.

There are two main types of printer used with most personal computers, the *inkjet* and the *laser*. Many of these are called MFPs (multifunction printers) as they combine in one device the roles of printer, photocopier and scanner. Scanning allows you to input or "digitize" an existing document which might consist of pages of text or pictures and photographs. Then the document can be saved on your hard disc or a flash drive, e-mailed to someone else or posted to a Web site.

Shown on the right is a typical multifunction inkjet printer. The lid on the top is shown in the raised position, ready for documents up to A4 size to be placed on the glass flat bed for scanning or copying.

Many printers have slots on the front which allow you to insert a memory card which has been removed from a digital camera.

Multifunction inkjet printer

Then the photos from the camera card can be input to the computer, edited on the screen, then saved on the hard disc drive before printing on paper.

Some inkjet printers are specifically designated as *photo printers*, but most inkjet and laser colour printers are capable of producing high quality prints. For best results, glossy *photo paper* is widely available from stationery shops, currently costing around £5 for a hundred 6x4 inch sheets, for example.

Printer Consumables

Many companies now offer quite serviceable inkjet printers at very modest prices, sometimes as low as £30. However, on top of this you must budget for replacement ink cartridges which can soon eclipse the purchase price of the printer, if you do a lot of printing. The inkjet colour printer usually has four cartridges, namely *cyan*, *magenta*, *yellow* and *black*. Prices vary greatly for different printers but you can easily pay over £30 for a set of four cartridges, unless you shop around on the Internet. For example, 3 sets of cartridges for the printer shown on the previous page were on offer for just £15 at the time of writing.

Colour and monochrome laser printers can be bought for under £100 and are faster than the inkjet, especially useful if you need to do large print runs. The cost of the toner cartridges for a laser printer ranges from about £30 — £100.

You can also buy cheaper *compatible* cartridges rather than the *original* versions from the printer manufacturer. Another option is to buy *refilled* cartridges or you can get a *refill kit* to do the job yourself. If you intend to do a lot of printing, the cost of the printing consumables is a big expense and it's worth investigating this thoroughly before buying a printer.

Installing a USB Printer

This is a task which anyone can accomplish. The basic methods are the same for most printers, but always read the user guide and instructions before unpacking and any light assembly such as the insertion of paper and cartridges, etc. There are usually only two cables — a power cable which plugs into a power point on the wall and a special *USB printer cable* which connects the printer to any one of the USB ports on the computer. The USB printer cable carries the data i.e. text and pictures, etc., from the computer to the printer, before printing on paper. As discussed later, you can also buy *wireless printers* which do not need to be connected to a computer via a USB printer cable.

Some manufacturers of devices such as printers advise you to install the software from their CD, before connecting the device to a USB port and switching on. This software CD contains programs called *device drivers*, necessary to make the device work properly with a particular version of the Windows operating system, such as Windows XP, Windows Vista or Windows 7.

If there are no contrary instructions from the manufacturers, simply switch the device on and plug it into any of the USB ports with the computer switched on and connected to the Internet. Windows detects the device and immediately tries to find the necessary drivers and install them. If the correct drivers are available they are downloaded from a Microsoft Internet service called *Windows Update*.

When a Brother USB printer was connected to a USB port on my Windows 7 laptop computer, the drivers were found and the installation proceeded automatically, as shown below.

 Installing device driver software
Click here for status.

If you select **Click here for status** as shown above, the following window appears displaying the progress of the driver installation.

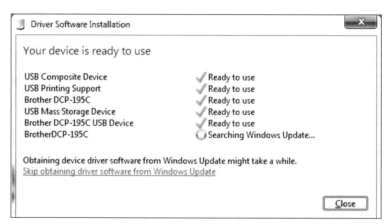

In my experience, Windows 7 usually finds the right device drivers for recent makes of printer. If Windows Update can't find the correct drivers you are advised to use the manufacturer's CD, if available. Finally, if all else fails, log on to the manufacturer's Web site where it should be possible to download the drivers to make the device work with your version of Windows.

Once the printer drivers have been installed you will see the message **Your device is ready to use**.

Checking the New Printer

You can find out a lot about the status of the printer by clicking the **Start** button at the bottom left of the screen and shown on the right. Then select **Devices and Printers** from the Start Menu. In this example, the **Brother DCP-195C** printer had just been installed as shown below.

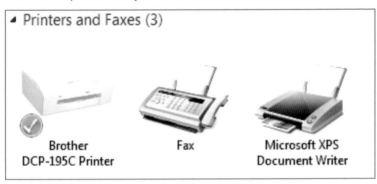

◢ Printers and Faxes (3)

Brother	Fax	Microsoft XPS
DCP-195C Printer		Document Writer

The tick above shows that the Brother is the *default printer*, i.e. the one which will be used automatically if you have more than one printer connected to the computer. If you right-click the icon for the printer, a menu pops up with options including setting a printer as the default printer or removing the printer drivers from the computer. Double-clicking the icon for the printer shown above displays another set of options including viewing the list of jobs in the *print queue* and cancelling print jobs if necessary.

An Overview of Microsoft Windows

The Evolution of Windows

The vast majority of personal computers in the world (around 90%) are operated using the suite of programs known as Microsoft Windows. Microsoft is probably the world's best known software company; the name Windows derives from the rectangular boxes in which programs and other features are displayed on the screen.

Early computers (back in the 1970s) were programmed by typing instructions in the form of lines of text at the keyboard, as shown on page 3; this was a complex task and best left to specialist programmers. Computers were eventually made more user-friendly by the development of *Graphical User Interfaces*, pioneered by companies such as Xerox and Apple Computers. Now you could simply use a mouse, a small hand-held pointing device, to select tasks listed in menus on the screen; other tasks were represented by small pictures or icons.

In 1985 Microsoft introduced Windows 1.0, its first operating system based on the more user-friendly graphical user interface. Since 1985 there have been several versions of Windows, such as Windows 3.1, Windows 98 and Windows XP. In 2007 Windows Vista was introduced with many new features. This was followed in 2009 by Windows 7, incorporating many of the lessons learned from earlier versions of Windows. A selection of sample icons from Windows 7 is shown below. These are discussed in more detail shortly.

What is Windows?

As mentioned previously, Windows 7 is a suite of programs (or sets of instructions) which control the computer; the first you see of it is when the computer starts up and you are presented with the main background screen known as the *Windows Desktop*.

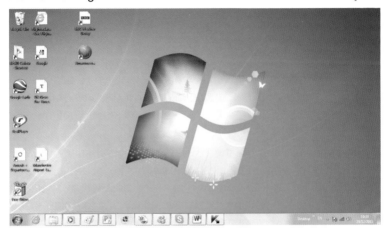

Shown above is the Desktop for Windows 7, the latest version of Microsoft Windows. As discussed in the next chapter, it's possible to customise the Desktop with different colour schemes and various designs for the background, known as "wallpapers".

Also shown on the left of the window above are various icons or *shortcuts* giving quick access to frequently-used Web sites, programs and folders containing documents.

The Desktop is the starting point for most computing sessions. Along the bottom of the Desktop is the *Taskbar*, shown below. On the extreme left of the Taskbar is the *Start* button, shown on the right, used for launching programs. Programs currently running appear as icons on the Taskbar, as shown below. Icons for frequently-used programs can be permanently "pinned" to the Taskbar.

Functions of Microsoft Windows

Some of the main functions of the Windows operating system are listed below:

- Provide the "point and click" graphical user interface consisting of windows, icons and menus on the screen.

- Enable the user to alter the appearance of the screen by changing colour schemes, "wallpaper", etc.

- Control the running of *applications*, launched by the user from the Start Menu, such as programs to draw pictures, edit photographs or compose music, etc.

- Manage the installation of hardware and software.

- Manage the permanent storage of documents and other work created by the user, by saving on the computer's internal hard disc drive or on removable media such as writeable CD/DVDs or USB flash drives.

- Enable the computer to communicate with peripheral devices such as printers and scanners.

- Provide *utility software* to maintain the computer .

- Provide a *browser* to search for and display Web pages. (Also to provide access to alternative browsers).

- Manage a home network which links two or more computers for sharing data files. Also enable the sharing of an Internet connection via a wireless router.

- Provide security systems to safeguard information and prevent malicious or criminal access to a computer.

- Provide **Ease of Access** facilities to help people with special needs to use the computer.

- Use a feature known as **Windows Update**, to download from the Internet modifications to the Windows software and also *device driver* software.

Advantages of Windows 7

This version of Microsoft Windows has been developed after taking into account feedback from users, based on their experience with earlier versions such as Windows XP and Vista. As a result, Windows 7 addresses many of the shortcomings of the earlier operating systems and has been greeted with critical acclaim. Some of the advantages of Windows 7, compared with Windows Vista and earlier systems are:

- The screen layout is simpler, less cluttered and with larger icons. The general design is more stylish.

- Searching for documents and other files is faster.

- The user can tailor Windows 7 to match their needs, so that frequently-used programs can be launched easily.

- The computer starts up and shuts down faster.

- Tests using the same computer have shown that Windows 7 performs tasks faster than Windows Vista.

- Windows 7 requires a less powerful computer than Vista and can be used with small netbook computers.

- Windows 7 has been found to work well with older designs of software and hardware such as printers. In the past, new operating systems have often been incompatible with older equipment because essential new software drivers were not available.

- Sharing files across several computers in a home network has been simplified.

- Windows 7 supports touch-screen operation. (This requires a special monitor or screen.)

- Users of Windows 7 have a choice of freely-downloadable Web browsers as an alternative to Internet Explorer, such as the popular Mozilla Firefox.

Windows Applications Software

As discussed earlier, Windows is primarily a program for managing and controlling the computer itself. However, separate programs are required for tasks such as producing a letter or editing a photograph, for example; some of this software may already be installed on a new computer, otherwise it is normally bought on a CD/DVD and installed, i.e. copied onto your computer's hard disc drive. Some software can also be *downloaded* from the Internet. Programs designed to perform these specific tasks are known as *applications software*, well-known examples being the word processor Microsoft Word and the Adobe Photoshop Elements photo editing program. All of these applications are launched by the user and run under the control of Windows, which is ever-present in the background.

Windows Paint

The Windows operating system itself contains some applications; these include the Windows Paint program shown below, which can be used for tasks such as drawing, painting, cropping photographs and saving images in different formats, for example.

WordPad

There is also a text-processor in Windows, known as WordPad, which contains many of the features of a word processor, used for formatting and editing documents, as shown below.

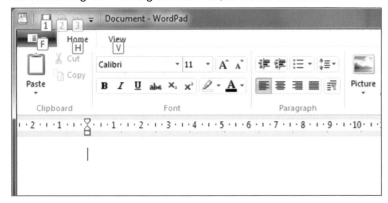

Notepad is another text processor included in Windows and used for creating very simple documents.

Windows Media Player

The Windows Media Player allows you to enjoy your favourite music while you are working on the computer; music and videos may be organised into different categories in your media library.

Windows Live Mail

Earlier versions of Windows contain built-in e-mail software; Windows XP includes the Outlook Express program and Windows Vista has Windows Mail. Windows 7 does not include its own e-mail program. However, a new version of Windows Mail, known as Windows Live Mail, shown below, can be freely downloaded from the following Microsoft Web site:

http://explore.live.com/windows-live-esssentials

Windows Live Essentials

Windows Live Mail shown above is part of a suite of software known as Windows Live Essentials, shown below. The Live Esssentials include programs for importing and editing photographs and videos, writing a *blog* or online diary, and "chatting" using text, voice and video messages.

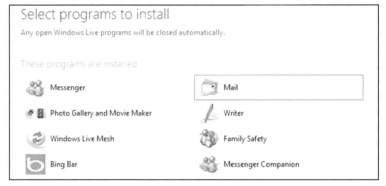

Internet Explorer

Included with Microsoft Windows is the Internet Explorer Web browser. This is a program used to display Web pages, as shown below in an extract from the **MSN TECH & GADGETS** page.

In earlier years Microsoft Windows included a built-in copy of Internet Explorer as the default Web browser. Third party Web browsers such as Mozilla Firefox and Google Chrome were also available and some people installed these to replace Internet Explorer. However, some manufacturers of rival Web browsers felt that Internet Explorer had an unfair advantage, since Explorer was already an integral part of the Windows operating system, installed on 90% of the world's personal computers. To overcome these objections from other browser manufacturers, Microsoft agreed to offer European users a *Browser Choice* window. This gives information on the various browsers and simplifies the task of downloading and installing them on your computer, as discussed later in this book. However, Internet Explorer is still the most widely used Web browser.

Bing shown above is Microsoft's own Internet *search engine*. This is a program used to find information by typing keywords into the Search Bar. Many people use *Google* as their preferred search engine and this is discussed later in this book.

Using the Internet

The diverse uses of the Internet alone must surely justify the expense of buying a computer. Nowadays there are cheap laptop, netbook and tablet computers which are quite capable of surfing the net. Some of these are available for under £200 and are ready to go online straight out of the box. Just a few of the many varied uses of the Internet are shown below.

- Sending e-mails to keep in touch with friends and family.
- Joining social networks such as Facebook and Twitter.
- Booking holidays after checking vacancies and viewing the accommodation and surrounding area, online.
- Live tracking of flights on your screen, also monitoring arrivals and departures at airports and checking in online.
- Completing income tax self-assessment online.
- Ordering the weekly shopping in just a few minutes.
- Using an online census to research your ancestors.
- Ordering books online, often delivered the next day.
- Selling surplus household items on eBay.
- Downloading software, music and ebooks.
- Finding excellent quality information about any subject.
- Comparing interest rates on Internet bank accounts.
- Checking current account bank statements, setting up standing orders and transferring funds online.
- Searching for property to buy or rent all over Britain.
- Ordering repeat prescriptions from the local surgery.
- Obtaining state pensions information and forecast online.
- Solving obscure crossword clues.
- Sending electronic animated greeting cards or e-cards.

Light Relief — Windows Games

If you need to relax after serious computing tasks like monitoring your cost of living on the Excel spreadsheet program or surfing the Internet for bargain prices, you can unwind by playing a few games on the computer. Windows provides a selection of games and they are all free and ready to launch; simply click the Start Button shown on the right then select **Games** from the right-hand side of the Start Menu.

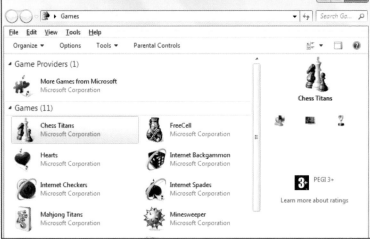

As shown above, **Chess Titans** is a computer version of chess in which you can play against another person or pit your wits against the computer. There are virtual card games such as **FreeCell** and **Solitaire** and traditional favourites such as **Minesweeper**.

If you need some company then you can play *online* games across the Internet with other people. These include **Internet Backgammon**, **Internet Checkers** and **Internet Spades**.

Some games have various levels such as beginner, intermediate and advanced. Click **Help** on the game's window to find the rules and instructions for playing the game.

Upgrading to Windows 7

If you are buying a new computer, you can ignore this section, because Windows 7 will already be installed. If you have an existing computer with an earlier version of Windows such as XP or Vista installed, there are many advantages to be gained by upgrading to Windows 7, as discussed on page 72. It's not a very difficult task to install Windows 7, to replace an earlier version of Windows. You simply buy a copy of Windows 7 on a DVD, insert the disc in the drive, follow the instructions on the screen and wait for it to be installed onto your computer's hard disc.

Minimum Computer Requirements for Windows 7

In order to run Windows 7 you need a modern computer with *1GB (gigabyte)* of *RAM* or *memory* and a *processor* with a speed of *1Ghz (gigahertz)*. There should also be *16 GB* of available space on the *hard disc*. The computer should be compatible with a graphics software standard known as DirectX 9.

Most modern computers, (including very small netbooks), comfortably meet the requirements for running Windows 7.

Editions of Windows 7

There are several editions of Windows 7, including Windows 7 Home Premium and the more expensive Windows 7 Professional and Windows 7 Ultimate. The last two have extra security and networking features intended for the professional user.

The Windows 7 Home Premium Family Pack allows you to use a single DVD to install Windows 7 on up to 3 machines. There are two DVDs in the Windows 7 package, known as 32-bit and 64-bit. The 64-bit edition can give improved performance on computers if they have the required high technical specification.

The 32-bit version of Windows 7 Home Premium should suffice for most home users.

Installing Windows 7

Before starting the installation, decide whether to use the 32-bit or 64-bit version of the software. Most home users of Windows XP should probably use the 32-bit disc. In Windows Vista, click **Start**, **Computer** and **System properties**. The current operating system, 32-bit or 64-bit, appears next to **System type:**.

Before inserting the Windows 7 DVD, make backup copies of your important data files onto a CD/DVD, external hard disc or flash drive. You will also need any *product keys* which were supplied with the software. Close any programs currently running and temporarily disable your anti-virus software. This can be done after right-clicking the icon for the anti-virus program on the right of the Windows Taskbar. Now place the Windows 7 disc in the drive, open the software and double-click **setup.exe**.

Upgrade or Clean Install

If you are running Windows Vista, you can select **Upgrade** when asked **Which type of installation do you want?** This will keep all of your existing files and software intact. If Windows XP is your current operating system, select **Custom** to carry out a **Clean** install, effectively replacing all of your installed programs and files on the hard disc. Programs such as Microsoft Word and Excel will need to be re-installed from the original CDs and DVDs, etc., once Windows 7 is up and running.

Now follow the instructions on the screen. You will be asked to enter the 25-character Windows 7 product key at some stage. The installation process may take two hours or more.

Compatibility of Windows 7 with Existing Software

I have installed Windows 7 on several computers as an upgrade to Windows Vista. This has always gone very smoothly, with few problems. It was, however, necessary to log on to a printer manufacturer's Web site to download their latest *device drivers* for Windows 7. Also to download the Windows 7 version of the Kaspersky Internet Security program from their Web site.

Working with Windows

The Windows Desktop

After the computer starts up, you are presented with the Windows Desktop, as shown below.

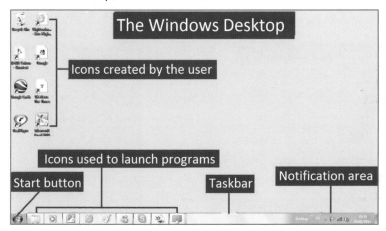

The Windows Desktop

Icons created by the user

Icons used to launch programs

Start button

Taskbar

Notification area

The horizontal bar across the bottom of the screen is known as the *Taskbar*. The *Start* button shown on the right and on the extreme left of the Taskbar above leads to the *Start* menu and the *All Programs* menu.

These two menus list the programs available on the computer. Programs can be launched using various methods, as follows:

- Click the name of the program in the Start menu.

- Click the name of the program in the All Programs menu.

- Click an icon for the program on the Windows 7 Taskbar.

- Double-click an icon on the Windows Desktop.

  (Creating icons for programs is discussed shortly).

The Start Menu

The Start menu shown below is launched by clicking the Start button shown on the right. The Start button is located at the bottom left of the screen. The left-hand panel of the Start menu lists recently used programs.

The programs listed on the left of the Start menu on the previous page include Windows' own programs such as **Paint** and **Windows Live Mail**. Other software, such as **Word 2010** and **Excel 2010** must be bought and installed separately. Recently opened programs appear automatically on the Start menu and you can also "pin" programs to the Start menu or remove them. The items listed on the right of the Start menu shown on the previous page are shortcuts to important Windows features such as **Computer** and **Control Panel**. These are used for managing and setting up the computer and are discussed shortly.

Shutting Down

Near the bottom right of the Start menu is the **Shut down** button; this should be used before switching the computer off, to avoid damaging any open files, as discussed later in this chapter.

The All Programs Menu

This menu and its sub-menus list all the programs installed on a computer. It is launched by clicking **All Programs**, shown at the bottom of the Start menu on the previous page. Shown on the right is the **Accessories** sub-menu in the **All Programs** menu. The other installed programs can be revealed using the vertical scroll bar shown on the right.

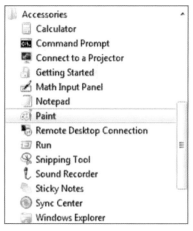

Some of the programs listed in the All Programs menu will be used rarely or not at all. Frequently used programs can be launched more quickly and easily after pinning them to the Start menu. Programs in regular use can also be launched with a single click from icons created on the Windows Taskbar, as discussed on the next page.

Launching Programs from the Taskbar

Any program can be launched by clicking its icon in the All Programs menu. However, if you use a program regularly, this is not the quickest method. For example, I use Microsoft Publisher a great deal. Windows 7 allows you to permanently "pin" an icon for a program onto the Taskbar at the bottom of the screen.

Pinning an Icon to the Taskbar or Start Menu

Select **Start**, **All Programs** and right-click over the program's name in the **All Programs** menu. Then select **Pin to Taskbar** or **Pin to Start Menu** as shown on the right. In the

> Open
>
> Troubleshoot compatibility
>
> Pin to Taskbar
>
> Pin to Start Menu

example below, the Microsoft Publisher icon has been pinned to the Taskbar as shown on the extreme right.

When a program is pinned to the Taskbar, it can be launched quickly with a single click. When a program is currently open and in use, its Taskbar icon is surrounded by a highlighted rectangle, as shown around the Publisher icon on the extreme right above.

If you launch a program from the Start menu or the All Programs menu, an icon for the program will appear on the Taskbar, surrounded by a rectangle. This temporary Taskbar icon will disappear when you close the program. To make an icon for a running program permanent on the Taskbar, right-click the icon and select **Pin this program to taskbar**. A pinned icon will stay on the Taskbar until you remove it by right-clicking the icon and clicking **Unpin this program from taskbar**.

To remove a program from the Start menu, right-click the name of the program and select **Unpin from Start Menu**.

Default Taskbar Icons

In the Taskbar extract shown on the previous page, three icons are shown to the right of the Start button. These icons are added by default and are always present, unless you choose to unpin them, as previously described. The three icons are as follows:

 Clicking this icon launches the Internet Explorer Web browser. (Alternative browsers are discussed later in this book).

 This icon opens Windows Explorer, which displays all your libraries of Documents, Music, Pictures, etc., and allows you to browse the hard disc, CDs/DVDs, etc.

 The Windows Media Player is launched by this icon, enabling you to play music and videos, organise your media into various categories and create playlists.

Thumbnails on the Taskbar

If you hover the cursor over a Taskbar icon for a program which is currently running, one or more small windows or *thumbnails* appear, displaying miniature versions of the full screen for that program. For example, hovering over the Internet Explorer icon displays thumbnails of any open Web pages, as shown below. If the thumbnail represents a Web page or a program currently running in the background, clicking anywhere on the thumbnail causes the Web page to open up fully on the screen.

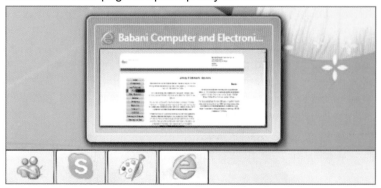

Jump Lists

These provide a very quick way of listing recently used documents, files and Web pages and then opening them on the screen. To open a Jump List, right-click over the icon for the relevant program on the Taskbar at the bottom of the screen.

Jump Lists and Documents

Shown on the right is the jump list obtained by right-clicking over the Microsoft Publisher icon on the Taskbar, shown on the left. Listed under **Recent** are documents I have been working on in the last few days. A single click on a document name such as **Computer Essentials** opens the document, filling the screen. There is also an option to unpin the icon for the **Microsoft Publisher** program from the Taskbar. **Close window** at the bottom shuts the program down.

If you right-click over a document in the list, there is an option to pin the document permanently to the Jump List. The document **Computer Essentails.pub** has been pinned to the Jump List, as shown on the right.

Jump Lists and Folders

 If you right-click the Windows Explorer icon shown on the left, a Jump List appears containing the names of folders you visit frequently. A single click opens the folder to reveal the files within.

Jump Lists and Web Sites

The Jump List on the right below was obtained by right-clicking the Internet Explorer icon on the Taskbar, shown on the left.

 The **Google** Internet search program shown on the right can be launched from this Jump List with a single click.

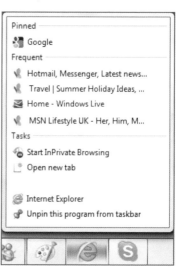

Listed under **Frequent** on the Jump List on the right are the names of Web sites which have been visited recently. A single click opens a Web site. Clicking **Start InPrivate Browsing** shown on the right above stops Internet Explorer from saving information about your browsing activities, such as your browsing History and Temporary Internet Files.

Open new tab in the screenshot above is used to open several Web sites simultaneously. *Tabs* allow you to switch quickly between Web sites. Three tabs are shown below in Internet Explorer. These are **Hotmail, Messenger,** etc., **Babani Computer and Electronic Books** and **AA Route Planner**.

The screen extract below shows the same three tabs in context across the top of a Web page in Internet Explorer 9. Tabs are discussed in more detail later in the chapter on Internet Explorer.

Displaying Windows in Different Ways

As discussed earlier, the icons on the left and middle of the Taskbar at the bottom of the screen are used for starting programs. Once a program starts running, its icon on the Taskbar is surrounded or highlighted by a rectangle.

The extract from the Taskbar above shows that two programs are currently running on this particular computer; these are Microsoft Publisher, indicated by the icon highlighted in a rectangle near the centre of the Taskbar and Windows Paint, with its palette icon highlighted on the right of the Taskbar.

Although you can have several programs up and running at a given time, normally only one of them is displayed in a window filling the whole screen, while the others run in the background.

In this example, Windows Paint is displayed in the foreground, occupying the whole screen. The Taskbar is always visible.

Maximizing, Minimizing and Closing Windows

Windows can be displayed in several different ways:

- Maximized so that they fill the whole screen.

- Minimized so that they only appear as icons on the Windows Taskbar across the bottom of the screen.

- As a thumbnail or miniature preview of the maximized window.

- Displayed at an intermediate size in between the size of the thumbnail and size of the maximized window.

A window which is currently minimized as an icon on the Taskbar can be restored to its original size by clicking the icon. Alternatively, allow the cursor to hover over the icon on the Taskbar and click the thumbnail which appears, as shown on the right.

A window which is currently open on the screen can be minimized by clicking the icon on the left of the three icons shown on the right. The middle icon either maximizes an intermediate size window or

restores a maximized window down to its original size. The cross icon on the right closes the window and shuts down the program.

Aero Shake

With several windows open, place the cursor in the top bar of a window you want to concentrate on. Hold down the left-hand button and shake the mouse. All other windows are minimized.

Displaying Two Windows Side by Side

It's often useful to have two windows open on the screen at the same time; for example, to make comparisons or to refer to information in one window while writing a report in the other. It's also easier to copy information from one window and "paste" it into the other when they are displayed simultaneously.

To display two windows side by side, place the cursor in the Title Bar across the top of the window. Keeping the left-hand button held down, drag the window to the left-hand edge of the screen until an outline of the window appears, then release the button. Now repeat the process by dragging the other window to the right side of the screen until the window's outline appears.

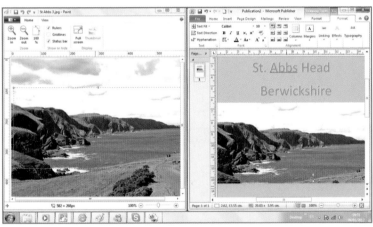

Windows Paint   *Microsoft Publisher*

In the above example, the Windows Paint program is running in its own window on the left of the screen, while the Microsoft Publisher DTP program is open in a window on the right. In the example above, part of a photograph displayed in Windows Paint in the left-hand window has been copied onto a page in Microsoft Publisher in the right-hand window. This was done using the **Copy** and **Paste** commands in Paint and Publisher.

The Notification Area of the Taskbar

As discussed earlier, the left-hand side and middle section of the Taskbar are mainly used for launching programs. On the far right of the Taskbar is a group of small icons and numbers, known as the *Notification Area* and shown below.

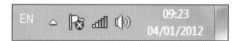

Viewing the Windows Desktop

You may wish to clear the Desktop, perhaps to launch a program from a Desktop icon, for example. Click the small **Show desktop** rectangle on the extreme right of the Taskbar; this clears the Desktop by "hiding" the currently open windows. Click the rectangle again to restore the windows to their previous size. Hovering the cursor over the rectangle gives a temporary view of the Desktop.

Language

EN on the Taskbar above shows that the language has been set to English on this particular computer. Right-click over **EN** to display a menu which allows you to change the language used.

Hidden Icons

To prevent cluttering the Taskbar, certain icons can be hidden. Clicking the small arrow shown on the left and on the Taskbar shown below reveals the hidden icons. These icons typically represent various utility programs such as anti-virus software and a program to manage the sound on the computer. Clicking **Customize...** shown on the right allows you to select which icons and notifications are to appear on the Taskbar.

Installing New Hardware

When your computer detects that a new piece of hardware has been attached to your computer, Windows has to install special software called *drivers*. You are informed of the progress of the installation process in the Notification Area as shown below.

Solve PC Issues

Clicking the small flag icon shown above and on the right gives notice of issues which require attention, such as a recommendation to use **Windows Backup** to make duplicate copies of important files. Or you might be advised to solve security issues or add anti-virus protection.

The Network Icon

This shows whether the computer is connected to the Internet and/or a local network. Clicking this icon leads to the Windows Network and Sharing Center, giving information about your computers and any networks they are connected to. If the computer is not connected but connections are available, an orange star appears over the network icon on the Taskbar, as shown on the right.

The Speakers Icon

Clicking this icon displays a slider which allows you to adjust the volume of your speakers; right-clicking the icon leads to various menus for setting the sound controls on your computer. These include the sounds emitted by the computer during various Windows operations, such as starting up, for example.

Date and Time

This is the final part of the Notification Area; clicking anywhere over the numbers opens up a full size calendar and a clock as shown on the right. All settings can be adjusted, including the International Time Zone, using **Change date and time settings....** Different months can be displayed on the calendar by clicking the arrows, as shown above either side of **January 2012**. To close the calendar, click anywhere outside of the window shown above.

Creating Icons on the Windows Desktop

You can place your own icons on the Windows desktop. These give rapid access or *shortcuts* to programs, Web sites or folders. To create an icon for a program, right-click over the program's name in the **All Programs** menu. Then from the pop-up menu select **Send to** and **Desktop (create shortcut)** as shown below. The same method is used to create an icon for a folder listed in the Windows Explorer.

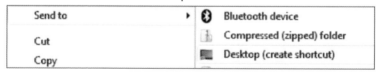

To create an icon for a Web page, right-click over the page and click **Create shortcut** from the pop-up menu. Then click **Yes** when asked if you want to place a shortcut on your Desktop.

To quickly open a program, Web page or folder, double-click the icon on the Windows Desktop, as shown by the three icons on the right.

The Control Panel

This important Windows feature is used for making changes to the settings for the hardware and software on the computer. The **Control Panel** is opened by clicking its name on the right-hand side of the Start menu, as shown below. (The programs listed below on the left-hand side are those recently used or pinned to the Start menu by the user and will vary on different computers).

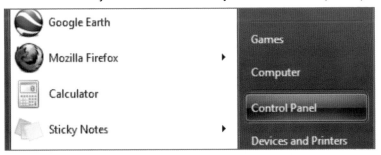

The **Control Panel** opens in its own window, as shown below in **Category** view.

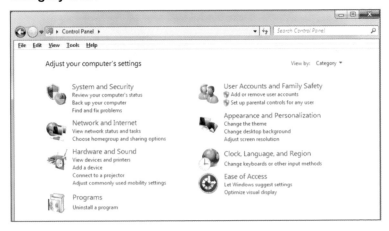

In **Category** view, the various tools to manage the computer's settings are grouped under main headings, such as **System and Security** and **Appearance and Personalization**, etc.

As can be seen on the previous page, the **Control Panel** has categories to manage all aspects of the computer, such as the security settings, changing the appearance of the windows and installing and removing hardware and software. **Ease of Access** shown on the previous page and discussed in the next chapter, allows you to set up your computer to provide help with any special needs such as impaired eyesight or reduced dexterity.

The view of the **Control Panel** can be changed by clicking the small arrow to the right of **View by: Category** shown on the right and on the previous page. This allows you to switch between **Category** view and **Large icons** and

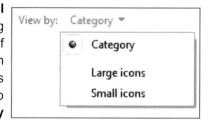

Small icons. The **Large icons** view is shown below, displaying approximately half of all the individual tools available in the **Control Panel**.

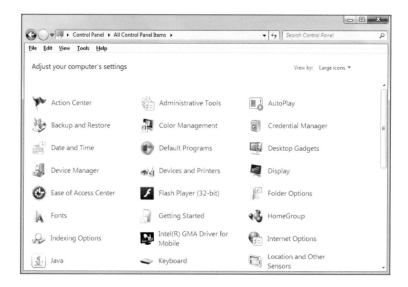

The Computer Window

The word **Computer** listed on the Start menu as shown below is the name of a special Windows folder.

Clicking **Computer** shown above opens up the following window displaying many of the resources on the computer.

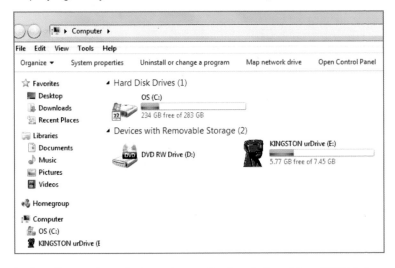

In the **Computer** window above, the hard disc drive **OS(C:)** has **234GB** free out of a total of **283GB**.

Kingston urDrive(E:) shown above is a flash drive or "dongle", a device which plugs into one of the USB ports (as described in Chapter 5). (When you attach a removable device such as a flash drive, external hard disc drive or digital camera, it appears in the **Computer** window with the next available drive letter, typically (E:) or (F:). Normally the hard disc drive is designated drive (C:) and the CD/DVD drive is (D:).)

The left-hand panel of the **Computer** window on the previous page lists all of your folders containing documents, music and video, etc., as well as the hard disc drive and any removable drives plugged into the USB ports.

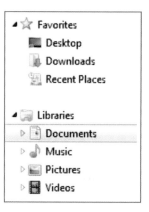

The **Libraries** are folders provided by Windows to save your documents, music and pictures, etc. Similarly, files downloaded from the Internet are automatically saved in the **Downloads** folder shown above.

Later in this book the creation of new folders with your own meaningful names is discussed. This makes it easier to return at a later date to a file representing a document or a picture, etc.

Several useful features appear across the top of the **Computer** window, as shown below.

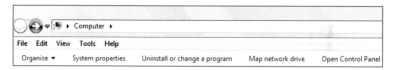

Clicking the arrow next to **Organize** shown above displays a menu including options to **Cut**, **Copy, Rename** and list the **Properties** of a file or folder in the **Computer** window.

System Properties shown above presents a window listing all the technical specification of the critical components in your computer, as discussed in more detail on page 47 of this book.

The Windows Explorer

This is a quick way to access the resources on your computer as an alternative to selecting **Computer** from the Start menu, as previously discussed. The Windows Explorer has an icon pinned to the Taskbar by default, as shown on the right and below.

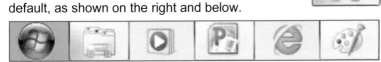

When you click the Windows Explorer icon shown above, the **Libraries** window opens. Clicking **Computer** in the left-hand panel then opens the **Computer** window as shown on page 96. This displays the various disc drives on the computer.

The Windows Explorer allows you to examine all the resources on your computer. Right-clicking over a folder or file opens a menu with options to carry out various tasks such as copying, deleting and renaming files and folders.

Removing Software Using the Computer Window

Uninstall or change a program listed on the **Computer** menu bar on the previous page is used to remove or uninstall software that you no longer need.

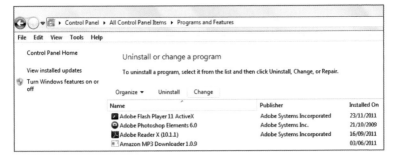

To remove a program, click its name in the list to select it, then click **Uninstall** from the middle menu as shown above. Some programs also have options to **Change** or **Repair** an installation.

If you have several computers, you may wish to connect them on a wireless network, as discussed later in this book. **Map network drive** in the extract from the **Computer** window shown below is used to create a shortcut to make it easier and quicker to share folders or computers on a network

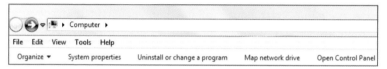

There is also an option in the **Computer** window shown above, to open the **Control Panel**, discussed in detail on page 94.

Removing Software Using the Control Panel

An option to uninstall a program also appears in the **Category** view of the **Control Panel** as shown on the right. Clicking this option leads to the **Programs and Features** Window shown at the bottom of the previous page.

Removing Programs Using the All Programs Menu

Some third party software includes an **Uninstall** option in its listing in the **All Programs** menu discussed on page 83. Shown below is the **Uninstall** option for **Google Chrome** in the **All Programs** menu. Google Chrome is a Web browser, a program used for finding and displaying Web pages. Google Chrome is a popular alternative to the Internet Explorer browser, along with Mozilla Firefox, as described elsewhere in this book.

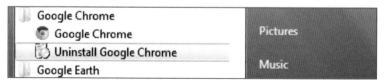

Click **Uninstall Google Chrome** shown above to begin the process to remove the software.

Shutting Down Correctly

Before shutting down the computer, save any documents or other files that you've been working on. If you have a document open in a program, such as a report in a word processor, this should be saved using **File** and **Save** from the program's menu.

Now click the **Start** button at the bottom left of the screen, as shown on the right, and click **Shut down**, as shown below, to close all open programs, shut down Windows and turn off the computer.

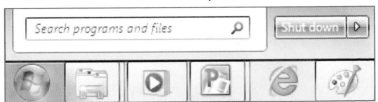

If you click the small arrow to the right of the **Shut down** button, the small menu shown on the right appears. **Switch user** and **Log off** might be used if several people have user accounts on this computer.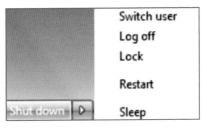

Restart shown above closes all programs, shuts down Windows and then starts the computer with Windows running again. You are often asked to **Restart** the computer in order to complete the installation of new hardware and software. The **Sleep** option (and also the **Hibernation** option used on some computers, especially laptops) puts the computer into a low power mode which saves electricity. All your work and settings are saved and later you simply press the power button to resume work where you left off.

*Always use the **Shut down** button to end a computing session. Simply switching the computer off may damage important files.*

8

Personalizing Windows

Changing the Appearance of Windows

Microsoft Windows allows you to change the background of your Desktop and also the colours used in the windows themselves. Right-click over the Windows Desktop and then select **Personalize** from the menu which appears. You can then choose from a number of ready-made themes, as shown below.

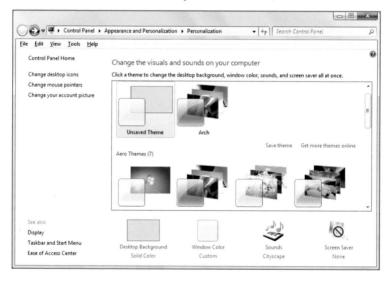

Each theme provides a design for the Desktop Background, different colour schemes for the windows and various sounds which accompany different Windows operations. Click the required icon to apply a theme to the Windows Desktop.

Alternatively the Desktop Background, colour of windows and the screen saver can each be changed separately, as described on the following pages.

Changing the Desktop Background

From the **Personalization** window shown on the previous page, select **Desktop Background**, as shown below.

As shown in the Desktop Background window below, there are several alternative ways of providing the background. The source of your Desktop Background is selected from the drop-down menu which appears after clicking the arrow to the right of **Picture location:** shown below.

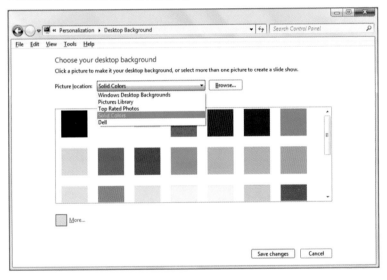

The **Desktop Background** window above shows the choice of colours available when the **Solid Colors** option is selected.

If you choose Windows Desktop Backgrounds, several sets of ready-made pictures are displayed, as shown on the next page.

As shown above, if you select more than one picture they can be viewed as a slide show, changing at regular time intervals as set by the user. Or you can click **Clear All** and then just select one picture and use this as your Desktop Background as shown below. Click the **Save changes** button shown above to make the new Desktop Background permanent.

Using Your Own Pictures for the Desktop

One or more of your own photographs or designs can be used as the Desktop Background; several photographs can be displayed as a slide show, providing a Desktop which changes at regular intervals. From the **Personalization** window shown on page 101, select **Desktop Background**, also shown on the next page, to open the window shown below.

Click the **Browse...** button shown above and then select the folder on your computer which contains your own pictures. In this example the pictures are in a folder called **Jills photos**. Now make sure there is a tick in the top left-hand corner of each picture you want to use. If you select more than one picture, i.e. to create a slide show, you can set the time each picture is displayed under **Change picture every:**. Switching the **Shuffle** option on with a tick changes the order of the pictures in the slide show each time it is displayed. Finally click **Save changes**.

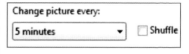

Changing the Colour of Windows

You can change the colour of the Taskbar, the Start Menu and the borders around windows after clicking **Window Color** from the **Personalization** window shown below and on page 101.

| Desktop Background | Window Color | Sounds | Screen Saver |
| Solid Color | Custom | Cityscape | None |

A grid appears as shown below, allowing you to choose the colour to be used in your Start Menu, Taskbar and borders of the windows. The slider allows you to adjust the colour intensity.

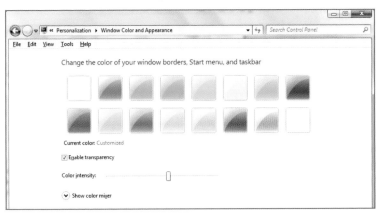

In the Desktop example on the right, the window colour has been set at **Fuchsia** and this is automatically applied to the Start Menu, Taskbar and any window borders. Here a photograph of our cat, Bop, is used for the Desktop Background.

Setting Up a Screen Saver

Screen savers were originally intended to protect the screen when the computer was switched on but not being used for long periods. Instead of a single screen image displayed continuously (and possibly damaging the screen itself) the screen saver presented either a blank display or a continually changing pattern. Modern monitors are less susceptible to damage from a constant display and screen savers are now used more for entertainment or privacy.

Right-click over the Desktop and select **Personalize** from the menu which pops up. The **Personalization** window is displayed, as shown on page 101. Now select **Screen Saver**, as shown on the right.

The **Screen Saver Settings** window allows you to select from a list of readymade patterns or use your own photos from the **Windows Live Photo Gallery** as shown above. Click the small arrow on the left of **Settings...** to see more screen saver options. You can also set the time to wait before the screen saver is activated.

Windows Gadgets

Gadgets are small windows which you can launch on the screen as an aside to your main on-screen activity, such as Web browsing, for example; the gadgets may provide information such as the time, currency exchange rates, the weather or news headlines, for example.

To display the choice of gadgets shown below, right-click over the Desktop and select **Gadgets** from the menu shown on the right.

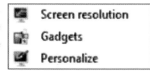

If you can't find a suitable gadget, more are available after clicking **Get more gadgets online** at the bottom right of the window shown above.

Displaying a Gadget

To display a gadget, double-click its icon, such as the **Weather** for example, shown on the right and in the window on the previous page. A small window appears, initially showing the weather for the London area, as shown below

right. If you hover the cursor over the gadget, the small vertical bar shown on the right of the gadget appears. The cross at the top of the bar closes the gadget. The small arrow enlarges the gadget as shown below, while

clicking the spanner icon presents various options. In this example you can select a different location for the weather forecast. For the clock gadget, the options allow you to change the Time Zone. There are eight different designs of clock to

choose from. A gadget can be moved to any position on the screen by placing the cursor over the gadget, holding down the left-hand mouse button and dragging the gadget to the required position.

Further options can be obtained by right-clicking over the gadget on the screen, then selecting from the menu which appears, as shown on the right.

A gadget is also available to display a slide show of your favourite pictures in a small window on the screen.

The Calculator

You can display a mouse-operated calculator on the screen. If you can't see **Calculator** listed in the Start Menu, click **Start**, **All Programs** and the **Accessories** sub-menu as shown below.

Click **Calculator** from the **Accessories** menu shown above and the calculator appears on the screen as shown below. It's just like a physical calculator, except that * (asterisk) and / are used for multiply and divide respectively.

An icon for the calculator appears on the Taskbar while the calculator is running, as shown below. If you expect to use the calculator regularly, right-click the icon on the Taskbar and select **Pin this program to taskbar**, as shown below. The calculator can then be launched whenever you need it by a single click of its icon, which is now residing permanently on the Taskbar.

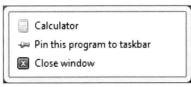

Setting the Screen Resolution

The screen display on your monitor is made up of a grid of small dots, known as *pixels, or picture elements*; a typical resolution for an LCD or flat screen monitor is 1280 x 1024 pixels, in the horizontal and vertical directions respectively. Windows normally sets the resolution to the optimum for a particular monitor, but you can experiment with different settings to suit yourself. At the higher resolutions some people will find the text too small.

Right-click over the Windows Desktop and select **Screen resolution** from the menu which appears, as shown on the right. Click the small downward pointing arrow to the right of the **Resolution** bar. Then drag the slider as shown on the right to experiment with different settings. You will need to click **Apply** and **OK** then **Keep changes** to make the changes permanent. The **Screen resolution** window also has an option **Make text and other items larger or smaller** allowing you to make the screen easier to read.

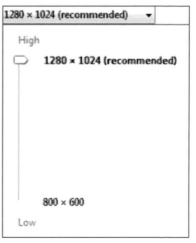

To get the best colour display on your screen, 32-bit colour is recommended. Setting the colour is done from the **Screen resolution** window by clicking **Advanced settings**, selecting the **Monitor** tab and making sure **True Color (32 bit)** appears under **Colors**, as shown on the right.

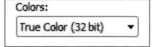

Help for Users with Special Needs

Windows provides a number of features to assist users with impairments such as defective eyesight, hearing difficulties or reduced manual dexterity. These features are found in the Ease of Access Center, which can be opened after clicking the Start button and selecting **Control** **Panel** from the right-hand side of the Start menu. As shown below, the **Control Panel** is

used for altering many of the software and hardware settings on the computer.

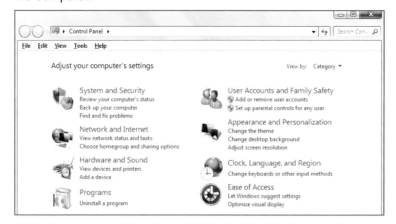

If you click **Ease of Access** shown above, a window opens displaying the options shown below. The **Ease of Access** **Center** contains the main tools to assist users with special needs. **Speech Recognition** allows you to "train" the computer to understand your spoken commands.

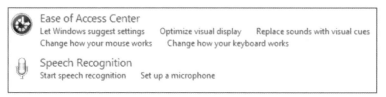

Clicking **Ease of Access Center**, shown at the bottom of the previous page, opens up the window shown below.

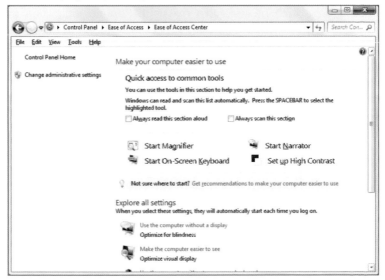

As shown above, there are four main features; these are the **Magnifier**, the **Narrator**, the **On-Screen Keyboard** and **High Contrast**, and these are discussed shortly. There are various approaches to begin using the **Ease of Access** features:

- If you know which feature you need, click its name, such as **Magnifier**, shown above, to launch the program.

- Answer a series of questions after clicking **Get recommendations to make your computer easier to use**. You may then choose to accept or reject the settings recommended for you by Windows.

- Work through a list of settings, as shown above under **Explore all settings** and decide which you want to use. This will allow you to switch on the narrator to read text on the screen, for example, or switch on the **On-Screen Keyboard**, if necessary.

Entering Your Own Special Needs

If you have any special needs, the **Ease of Access Center** allows you to input them by selecting from several lists of impairments. Then a list of recommended settings is produced which you can apply if you wish. Click **Get recommendations to make your computer easier to use**, halfway down the **Ease of Access Center** window, as shown on the previous page. You are presented with a series of statements under the headings **Eyesight**, **Dexterity**, **Hearing**, **Speech** and **Reasoning**. Each statement is preceded by a check box, which you can tick by clicking with the mouse if it applies to you. For example, some of the **Eyesight** statements are shown below:

Eyesight (1 of 5)

Select all statements that apply to you:

☑ Images and text on TV are difficult to see (even when I'm wearing glasses).

☐ Lighting conditions make it difficult to see images on my monitor.

☐ I am blind.

After you click **Next**, the investigation of your needs continues with the statements on **Dexterity**, **Hearing**, **Speech** and **Reasoning**. Finally a list of recommended settings is displayed which you may, if you wish, choose to switch on by clicking to place a tick in the check box, as shown below:

Recommended settings

These settings can help you set up your computer to meet your needs. Review th
below and select the options that you want to use.

☑ Turn on Narrator

Narrator reads aloud any text on the screen. You will need speakers.

☑ Turn on Magnifier

Magnifier zooms in anywhere on the screen, and makes everything in th
Magnifier around, lock it in one place, or resize it.

The list of **Recommended settings** shown previously may also include options to change the colour and size of the mouse pointers as shown below:

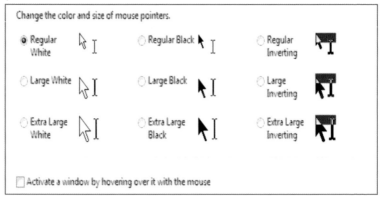

Another option is to **Turn on Sticky Keys**. Some keyboard *shortcuts* require three keys on the keyboard to be pressed simultaneously. **Sticky Keys** allow these operations to be reduced to a single key press.

Turn on Mouse Keys enables the numeric keypad (on the right of the keyboard) and also the arrow keys, to move the mouse pointer around the screen.

When you've finished selecting your **Ease of Access** recommended settings, click **Apply** and **OK** near the bottom of the screen. From now on, each time you start the computer, your chosen features, such as the **Magnifier** or the **On-Screen Keyboard**, will start up automatically.

At the bottom of the list of **Ease of Access** recommendations is a clickable link, shown below.

See also

Learn about additional assistive technologies online

This launches a Web site giving further information about *assistive technology* products for anyone with special needs.

Using the Magnifier

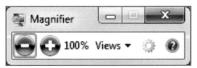

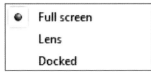

Click **Start Magnifier as** shown on page 112. The small **Magnifier** window opens, as shown on the right. Click the **+** or **–** signs to increase or decrease the size of the text on the screen. Click the small arrow on the right of **Views** above and you can choose whether to enlarge the **Full screen** or just a small moveable rectangular area around the cursor, known as the **Lens,** as shown below.

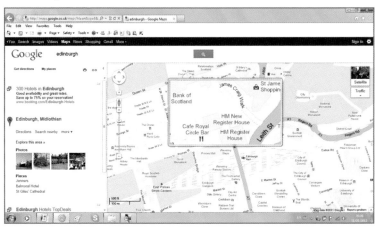

The **Docked** option shown near the top of the page displays the enlarged part of the screen in a separate window while simultaneously displaying the normal 100% view in its own window.

If the **Magnifier** is running but has not been used for a short time, it changes to an icon for a magnifying glass. Click this icon to display the **Magnifier** window again, as shown at the top of this page.

Using the Narrator

The **Narrator** reads out aloud the details of any windows you've opened, toolbars, menu options, the keys you've pressed and any text in documents on the screen. The **Narrator** is launched by clicking **Start Narrator** in the **Ease of Access Center**, as shown on page 112. After a few seconds the **Narrator** window appears, as shown below, allowing you to make various adjustments to the settings. When the **Narrator** is running, an icon is displayed on the Windows Taskbar, as shown on the right.

Press **Exit** to stop using the **Narrator**. More details about the **Narrator** can be found after clicking the Start button, then **Help and Support** and entering **Narrator** in the Search Bar.

The On-screen Keyboard

If you have trouble using an ordinary keyboard, you may find it easier to use the virtual keyboard provided in Windows. From the **Ease of Access Center** shown on page 112, select **Start On-Screen Keyboard**. An image of a keyboard appears on the screen as shown below. There is also an icon for the **On-Screen Keyboard** on the Windows Taskbar, as shown on the right.

The **On-Screen Keyboard** is operated by a mouse or other device, such as a joystick. Place the cursor where you want to begin typing and point to and click the required letters.

Upper case (i.e. capital) letters are obtained by first clicking one of the on-screen **Shift** keys shown above. The **On-Screen Keyboard** can be moved to a convenient position by dragging in the area to the right of the words **On-Screen Keyboard**.

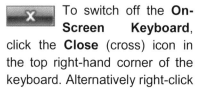 To switch off the **On-Screen Keyboard**, click the **Close** (cross) icon in the top right-hand corner of the keyboard. Alternatively right-click  the Taskbar icon and click **Close window** on the menu which pops up as shown above. To use the **On-Screen Keyboard** regularly, click **Pin this program to taskbar** as shown above

High Contrast

This option is intended to make the screen easier to read by increasing the contrast on colours. **High Contrast** is switched on and off by simultaneously pressing down **Alt** + left **Shift** + **PRINT SCREEN** (may be marked **Prt Sc** or similar on your keyboard).

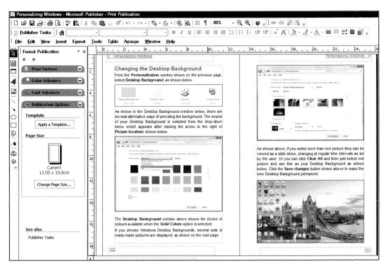

Shown above is the **High Contrast White** theme. There are several different **High Contrast** themes listed in the **Personalization** section of the **Control Panel** discussed on page 101. Right-click over the Windows Desktop and select **Personalize** from the menu which appears. Then scroll down and select one of the **Basic and High Contrast Themes** by clicking, as shown in the extract below.

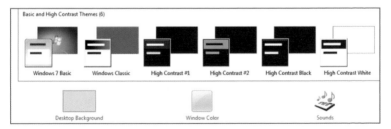

Speech Recognition

This feature allows you to control the computer by spoken commands. The necessary sound facilities are normally built into a laptop but on a desktop computer you may need to add speakers and a microphone. Tasks such as starting programs and opening menus, dictating text and writing and sending e-mails can be achieved without using a touchpad, mouse or keyboard at all. First you need to learn some spoken commands, by following the Windows **Speech Tutorial**; you must also "train" the computer to recognise your voice and dialect if you have one.

The feature is launched by clicking **Start**, **Control Panel** and, if the **Control Panel** is in **Category** view, selecting **Ease of Access** and then **Speech Recognition**.

If the **Control Panel** is in **Large icons** or **Small icons** view, click the **Speech Recognition** icon shown on the right. Then the **Speech Recognition** window opens, as shown below.

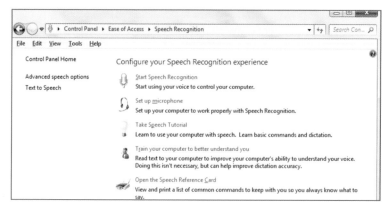

Experienced users can click **Start Speech Recognition** or beginners can select **Take Speech Tutorial** as shown above.

As shown on the previous page, there is a **Set up microphone** option. The program recommends a headset microphone for best results with speech recognition.

When you first start **Speech Recognition** you are given advice on the use of the microphone and you are asked to read in a piece of sample text. The **Speech Tutorial** helps you to practise all of the basic spoken commands such as **Start Listening**, **New Line**, **New Paragraph** and **Correct**. You are given practice at correcting mistakes on the screen and shown how to use voice commands to select menus such as **Start**, **All Programs** and **File** and to launch programs. Selecting **Train your computer to better understand you** shown on the previous page, launches extensive practice exercises in which you speak into the microphone, while the computer learns to recognise your voice.

After you've finished training yourself (and the computer) you are ready to click **Start Speech Recognition** as shown on the previous page; this displays the microphone user interface shown below:

The user gives commands such as **Start listening** to make the computer begin interpreting the commands spoken into the microphone. The microphone button shown on the left above changes colour – blue indicating that the computer is listening to you, grey indicating not listening. The small window in the centre gives text feedback such as **Listening** or **Sleeping**. The message **What was that?** shown in the text window below indicates that a command was not understood by the computer.

If this message appears, try giving the command again or try a new command. You can display a list of commands on the screen at any time by saying **What can I say?**, as shown below.

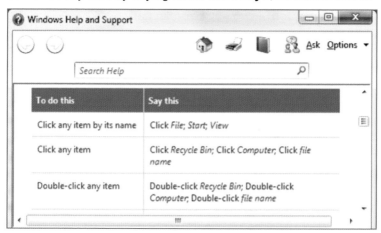

The spoken command **Show numbers** displays numbers which appear transparently over objects on the screen. For example, the **Show numbers** command might allocate the number **14** to a picture or photograph listed in the Windows Explorer. The spoken command **Double-click 14** would open the photograph in its associated program, such as Windows Paint or Adobe Photoshop Elements, for example.

The Speech Recognition feature allows anyone who can't manipulate a mouse, touchpad or keyboard to utilise programs such as Microsoft Word, or e-mail, for example. Using only spoken commands, you can create, edit, save and print documents. I have found it quite easy to use the Speech Recognition system to dictate fairly simple documents. However, it is important to work through the tutorials thoroughly and to spend plenty of time training the computer to recognise your voice. It also helps to speak slowly and clearly into the microphone. My own experience has confirmed that the headset microphone gives the best results for speech recognition.

Further Help

There are many companies and organisations offering specialist help, in addition to the tools available within Microsoft Windows as just discussed. For example, alternative input devices are available for sufferers of illnesses such as Parkinson's Disease or Cerebral Palsy. There is a useful link, shown below, at the end of the **Ease of Access Recommended settings**, as discussed on pages 113 and 114.

See also

Learn about additional assistive technologies online

Clicking this link enables you to access a wide range of information on assistive technology and accessibility issues.

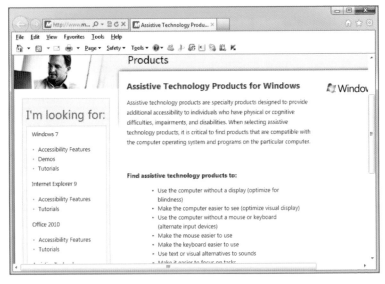

As well as exploring links to Web sites giving details of specialist devices, such as the **Head Mounted Mousing Alternative**, you might also carry out your own searches by entering keywords such as **disability computer technology** or **special needs computer equipment** into a search program such as Google.

Getting Online to the Internet

Introduction

In the last few years the Internet has become an essential part of the lives of many people and some of us probably wonder how we ever managed without it. With the increasing use of laptops, tablet computers and smartphones it's now possible to connect to the Internet whether you're at home or travelling abroad. In recent years *broadband* technology has enabled information to be delivered much faster via the telephone cables from the Internet to your computer. Some general categories of Internet activity are as follows:

- Searching for up-to-date information on any subject using a *search engine* (a program) such as Google, instead of a traditional encyclopaedia.

- Using specialist Web sites, e.g. to trace family history.

- *Communicating* electronically with other people worldwide using e-mail and social networks such as Facebook and Twitter to share text messages and photos. Also telephone calls with live video (Skype).

- *Shopping online* for virtually anything from one of the many online retailers. Also selling items on the eBay online auction Web site.

- *Downloading* music, videos, TV programmes and computer software from the Internet to your computer.

- Carrying out *online banking*, financial transactions and many form-filling tasks such as a Self-Assessment Tax Return and online applications such as Car Tax.

Broadband

For several years the only way home users were able to connect to the Internet was using a device called a *dial-up* modem; this linked the computer to an ordinary telephone line. In recent years a much faster system known as *broadband* has become the standard; this enables you to surf the Internet more quickly and download large files such as videos and music. These tasks were too time consuming using the earlier dial-up systems.

The latest high speed broadband service from BT, known as *BT Infinity*, uses *fibre optic* cables rather than the earlier copper wires. BT Infinity is only available in certain areas at the time of writing — you can find out if your home can get Infinity by logging on to **www.bt.com/infinity** and entering your telephone number.

Before you can connect to the Internet, the line to your home has to be *activated* by BT. You also need a special *ADSL modem* or a *router* to connect to a broadband Internet service.

If you already have access to an Internet computer, you can find out which broadband services are available in your area by logging on to **www.broadbandchecker.co.uk** and entering your postcode. An example of the results is shown below:

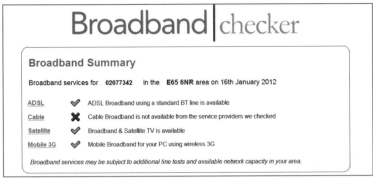

If you don't already have access to an Internet computer to find this information, you should be able to log on in a local library or Internet cafe.

Many people use the BT Broadband service while others use companies such as AOL and Tiscali, who deliver an Internet service over the BT phone lines. Virgin Media provide Cable Broadband to areas covered by cable television and Sky offer TV and Broadband via satellite. Some mobile phone companies provide *mobile broadband* using a dongle which plugs into a USB port on your computer, as discussed later in this chapter.

Internet Service Providers

Web sites such as **www.uswitch.com/broadband** allow you to enter your postcode and find the various competing offers from Internet Service Providers, as shown below.

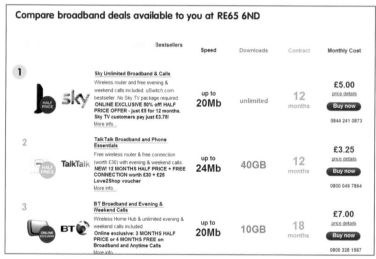

The cost of a 12 or 18 month contract may be anything from £3 to £30 a month. **Speed** is the *maximum* download speed — currently 20Mb or 40Mb (over fibre optic cables) are often quoted. (Mb or megabits means millions of bits or binary digits per second — bits are discussed on page 45). The **Download** figure above (e.g. 40GB) is the amount of data (pictures, video, etc.), you can download per month. A free wireless router worth about £50 is often included in a broadband package.

Broadband Requirements

The next few pages explain how to set up one or more computers to use an ADSL broadband service based on the BT telephone lines. The essential requirements are:

- An account with an Internet Service Provider such as BT, AOL or Tiscali, etc.

- A BT telephone socket and a telephone line which has been tested by BT and activated for ADSL broadband.

- A wireless router containing an ADSL modem. Many Internet Service Providers now include a free router as part of the package.

- One or more *filters* allowing a telephone socket to be used for broadband and phone calls at the same time .

- A cable to connect the router to the filter.

- An Ethernet cable to assist in the initial setup of the router to the computer.

- Laptop computers normally have their own built-in wireless networking capability. However, each desktop machine connected to the wireless router needs a *wireless network adaptor*. This may be in the form of a PCI expansion card fitted inside of the computer; alternatively the adaptor can be a *USB dongle* as discussed on page 56.

- Software and instructions for setting up the router, usually on a CD included in the start up package from the Internet Service Provider, such as BT.

- In the case of a wireless router, a *network name* and a *security key* to prevent other people from logging on to your Internet connection from outside of your home. (Wireless home networks may have a range of 100-300 feet, depending on obstructions like walls and floors.)

The Wireless Router

A wireless router with a built-in ADSL modem is one of the most popular ways of connecting to the Internet, even if you only have one computer. Many Internet Service Providers include a free router in their start up kit. If you have more than one computer, the wireless router can connect them all on a wireless network, using a single telephone socket. I have found a wireless network to be extremely reliable with several computers scattered about the house in different rooms.

The initial setting up of the router may require a computer to be sitting next to the router and connected to it by an Ethernet cable. However, once the network is up and running the wireless router can sit on its own next to your telephone socket, with no computers physically connected to it. Our router sits in the dining room next to the telephone socket, while the computers themselves are in different rooms around the house. The router requires virtually no attention except for switching off and on again about twice a year. This simple operation is an effective panacea for a wide range of complex computing problems.

A wireless router

The Wireless Router Startup Kit

If you subscribe to an Internet Service Provider such as BT, you may obtain a free wireless router and the various components needed to get you started, as shown below.

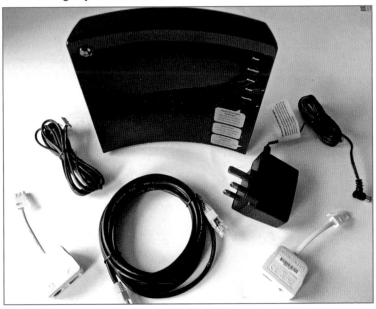

The BT Home Hub wireless router and accessories

In the above photograph, the router itself is the large black box at the rear. On the right is the power supply cable and transformer. The white cables and sockets are known as *filters* or *microfilters*; these plug into the main telephone socket(s) in your home. Each filter itself has two sockets; one socket connects an ordinary telephone handset while the other accepts the broadband cable from the router. This is the black cable shown to the left of the router above. The filter enables an ordinary telephone to be used at the same time as the broadband Internet.

The Router Ports in Detail

Shown below are ports on the rear of the wireless router supplied by BT as part of their broadband package.

The ports on the back of the BT Home Hub wireless router

The left-hand socket in the group above is used for the cable which connects the router to the broadband telephone socket, via a filter, as mentioned on the previous page. The green socket is for a special BT Internet telephone. The four yellow Ethernet sockets have several uses, such as the initial setting up of the router using an Ethernet cable connected to a computer. The Ethernet sockets can also be used to create a wired network, using Ethernet cables and adaptors instead of wireless technology. Wired networks are often preferred in business, since they can be faster than wireless and unsightly cables may not be such an issue as they are in a home environment.

On the right of the router above is the socket for the power cable; finally there is a USB socket to connect a USB cable to a USB port on a computer (as an alternative to an Ethernet cable.)

BT Vision

One of the Ethernet sockets on the router can be used to connect an Ethernet cable from the router to a BT Vision digital television box. This allows a large number of Freeview programs to be viewed and recorded; live television can be paused and restarted. A daily program guide can be downloaded and extra programs and films are available on demand, (for a fee).

Instruction Manuals

The router package should include an instruction manual and a quick-start leaflet; a more comprehensive manual may be provided on a CD which accompanies the router or alternatively on the router manufacturer's Web site.

Wireless Network Adaptors

Each computer on a wireless network must be able to communicate with the wireless router. Laptop computers are normally supplied with built in wireless networking capability. This facility may need to be switched on by a physical switch or by pressing a designated function key on the keyboard.

USB Wireless Dongle

Desktop computers may need to be fitted with a separate *wireless network adaptor,* in the form of a "dongle" which plugs into a USB port on the computer, as shown below.

A USB wireless network adaptor dongle

Installing a Wireless Router

Before you can start to set up a wireless network based on a wireless router, your telephone line must be tested and activated for ADSL broadband by BT. If you are using an Internet Service Provider other than BT, they may make the arrangements for you. You might have to wait a week or 10 days for the activation to be effective.

Once the telephone line is activated you can start installing the router. Ideally the router should be in a central position in your home if you are connecting several computers. If possible, avoiding installing the router near to a microwave oven or cordless phones as these may interfere with the broadband.

Place a filter in the main telephone socket in your home. If you want to use an ordinary telephone here, there is a socket for this on the filter. Now connect the special broadband cable (known as an RJ11 cable) from the router to the other socket in the filter. (The broadband and ordinary telephone sockets in the filter are quite different, so you can't connect the cables incorrectly.)

Now connect the power cable from a power point to the router and switch on. Initially the diagnostic lights on the front of the router will flash yellow and then after a minute or two the power, broadband and wireless lights should be constant blue.

Set up a computer within a few feet of the router. This computer should be fitted with a wireless network adaptor as discussed earlier. Most modern laptops have built-in wireless networking capability although this may need to be switched on. Some desktop computers are also "wireless ready" but otherwise they need a USB or PCI wireless adaptor fitted, as discussed earlier. BT provide an installation CD which is intended to be used on every computer, although this may not always be essential to make the connection to the Internet.

Start up the computer and the small Internet icon on the right of the Taskbar and shown here on the right will initially display a yellow star; hover the cursor over this icon and it should display the message **Not connected — Connections are available**. Click the Internet icon and a list of nearby wireless networks is displayed, including yours, as shown below:

In the above example, two networks have been detected; the name of a network such as **BTHomeHub-5778** is also referred to as the *SSID* or *Service Set Identifier*. Now click the name of your router, such as the **BTHomeHub** and then click the **Connect** button which appears.

You must then enter a *wireless key* to make the network secure. The BT security key is displayed on the back of the router and on a small card provided in the router package.

Entering the Security Key

The security key or password must be entered into every computer the first time it is connected to the router. If you don't have a secure network, any of your neighbours or someone nearby with a laptop could use your Internet connection and possibly hack into your data. The dialogue box for entering the security key is shown below.

After entering the security key, click **OK** and you should soon be told that you are connected to the Internet. The icon should now be clear of crosses or yellow stars as shown on the right and on the Taskbar at the bottom right of the screen. If you hover the cursor over this icon it should give the name of the wireless hub and confirm that

you have *Internet Access*, as shown below.

Using an Ethernet Cable to Connect a Router

An Ethernet cable, also known as an RJ45 cable, usually with yellow connectors at each end, should be supplied with your router kit. If you are unable, for any reason, to make a wireless connection to the Internet, the Ethernet cable provides a temporary direct link between your router and the computer.

Some routers, such as those made by Belkin and Linksys, require you to connect the computer with an Ethernet cable; then, using a Web browser such as Internet Explorer, type the *IP address* of the router, such as **192.168.2.1** for example, into the browser's address bar, as shown below.

This IP address will connect you to the router in the same way that an IP address can be used to connect to a Web page. You can now set up the router using settings provided by your Internet Service Provider. These might include a username and password and other details such as the type of wireless security, usually either WEP or WPA. These are methods of *encryption* which involves encoding information so that only people with a key can *decipher* it. Please see your router's instruction manual for the precise details for creating a secure network.

Once the router and each computer are set up, you can dispense with the Ethernet cables and connect to the Internet wirelessly.

With the BT Home Hub router discussed earlier it should not be necessary to connect the computer to the router using an Ethernet cable. This is because the BT Home Hub is already set up and often only requires the wireless key to be entered to make the connection. However, should there be any problems in connecting wirelessly, it might be helpful to plug in the Ethernet cable, connect to the Internet and login to your Internet Service Provider's Web site or router manufacturer to obtain online help.

Checking Your Internet Connection

Click the Internet icon at the bottom right of the screen, then from the window which pops up click **Open** **Network and Sharing Center**, as shown on page 133. This dialogue box, shown below, allows you to view many aspects of your new wireless network. You can also set up your network so that printers, files and other resources can be shared by all of the computers on the network, as discussed shortly.

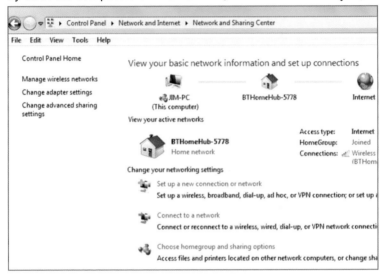

You can also check the speed of your broadband Internet connection. At the time of writing, many services offer a download speed of up to 10Mbps and a few offer up to 40Mbps. In practice this speed may not be achieved due to limitations such as your distance from the telephone exchange. You can check your speeds by logging onto a Web site such as:

www.broadbandspeedchecker.co.uk

The results of a speed test on one of my computers are shown on the next page.

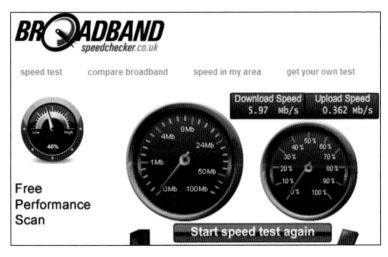

As can be seen above, my computer recorded a download speed of 5.97Mb (megabits per second) and an upload speed of 0.362Mb. I live on the same road as a telephone exchange which has been upgraded to provide BT Infinity 40Mb download speeds over fibre optic cables. The Web site **www.bt.com/infinity** lists reasons why some people may not be able to get BT Infinity, even if their telephone exchange has been upgraded. These reasons include your distance from the green roadside cabinets and perhaps the need to modify the cabinets themselves.

To check the availability of BT Infinity to your home, log on to **www.bt.com/infinity** and enter your landline telephone number.

Your broadband checker results

Broadband option	Broadband speed range	When you can get
BT Total Broadband ⑦	Between 7.5Mb and 17.5Mb (Estimated speed: 13.0Mb)	Now

Sorry, you're not currently able to get BT Infinity. This may be because your area has not been enabled yet, or your individual line does not support super-fast broadband. Register your interest and we'll let you know if this changes.

Summary: Getting Online Using a Router

The following list outlines the general method of connecting to the Internet using a BT ADSL broadband telephone line and a wireless router:

1. Check that you can receive ADSL broadband from your local telephone exchange.

2. Sign up with an Internet Service Provider.

3. Wait for BT or another company to test and activate your telephone line to receive broadband.

4. Obtain a wireless router with a built-in ADSL modem. Your Internet Service Provider may supply this.

5. Insert a microfilter into the main telephone socket in your home.

6. Insert the cable from a telephone handset into the telephone socket in the microfilter.

7. Connect the broadband cable from the router into the broadband socket in the microfilter.

8. Connect the power lead for the router and switch on. The power light on the router should be on; then the wireless and broadband lights should stop flashing.

9. Set up a "wireless enabled" computer near to the router. If necessary attach an RJ45 Ethernet cable between the router and the computer.

10. Start up the computer and connect to the Internet using a Web browser such as Internet Explorer. Enter the wireless key and/or any other information for your router or supplied by your Internet Service Provider.

11. Remove the Ethernet cable and repeat steps 9 and 10 for any other computers on the network.

12. You should now be able to connect wirelessly to the Internet from any computer on the network.

Internet Connections on the Move

You may want to connect to the Internet when you're away from home. For example, to keep in touch with your family or work colleagues or to check flights and train times. Modern laptop, netbook and tablet computers make getting online away from home a relatively cheap and simple operation.

Wireless Hotspots

Hotels, airports, etc. have *wireless hotspots* or Internet access points. When you're within range (up to 100ft indoors, say), a laptop can detect the router at the access point. To connect to the Internet, just enter the password provided by the establishment. In some cases you enter your mobile phone number and the password is sent back to your phone in a text message. There may be a charge to use the access point. Alternatively many hotels allow you to plug an Ethernet cable (discussed on page 53) from your laptop into their wired network.

Mobile Broadband

3G or 3rd Generation is a telecommunications standard which applies to mobile phones or smartphones capable of connecting to the Internet. Many of the mobile phone companies enable you to connect a computer to the Internet using the 3G mobile phone network. The company provides you with a SIM card (Subscriber Identity Module) containing information to connect you to the Internet. They may also provide a *mobile broadband dongle* (shown on the right) which plugs into one of the USB ports on the computer, as discussed on page 54. The dongle has a slot into which you slide the SIM card. Some computers, such as tablets, have a built-in slot for a SIM card, so that a dongle isn't needed.

3 Mobile broadband dongle

As with mobile phones, there is a wide choice of pay-as-you-go and fixed term contracts for mobile broadband. If you already have access to the Internet, try typing **mobile broadband** into a search engine such as Google or Bing to see what's on offer.

For example, I bought a pay-as-you-go dongle for the 3 (**Three.co.uk**) network for under £20. Mobile broadband pay-as-you-go services typically include 30 days preloaded credit, after which you pay to top up. Contracts might cost £8-£15 per month for 12 or 18 months. For a tablet computer, the SIM card may be provided on its own, to be inserted directly into the tablet.

To get online with a dongle, slide the SIM card into the dongle and plug the dongle into one of the USB ports on the computer, as discussed on page 54. The installation process will probably be automatic but it's always advisable to follow any instructions on the screen and in the installation guide. On completion an icon for the new mobile broadband Internet connection may appear on the Windows Desktop. You should now be able to use your computer to connect to the Internet from wherever there is an adequate signal for your chosen phone network. The 3 network dongle uses a short USB cable to improve the signal.

Apart from laptops on the move, a mobile broadband dongle can be used to connect to the Internet any computer with a USB port, including a stationary desktop machine.

Installing a Printer on a Wireless Network

The wireless router allows several computers in your home to share an Internet connection through a single telephone socket. The wireless router also enables a *network* to be created so that computers anywhere around the home can communicate with each other and share resources such as files and printers.

For the home or small business with more than one computer, the ability to share a printer on a wireless network is very useful. This is obviously cheaper than having a separate printer connected to each computer. As discussed below, to share a printer on a network you need to switch on the **File and Printer Sharing** option and also make the printer itself *shareable.*

Turning on File and Printer Sharing

This option may already be switched on, but it's a simple task to make sure anyway. Open the **Network and Sharing Center** as described on page 135 and from the left-hand panel select **Change advanced sharing settings**.

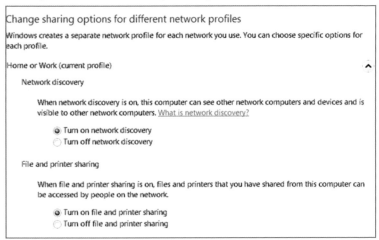

Make sure **Turn on file and printer sharing** is selected as shown above, then click the **Save changes** button.

Making a Printer Shareable

A printer is usually attached to one of the computers on a network via a USB cable. Setting up a printer in this way was discussed in Chapter 5. The other computers on the network can then connect to this printer wirelessly.

First the printer has to be *shareable* so that other computers can use it. Using the computer attached to the printer, click the **Start** button in the bottom left-hand corner of the screen. From the Start Menu select **Devices and Printers** as shown below.

The **Devices and Printers** window opens showing the default printer marked with a tick. (The default printer is the one used automatically when you print a document. Some printers listed in **Devices and Printers** may be shared network printers, not physically connected to the computer you are working at.)

Right-click over the printer icon similar to the one shown at the bottom of the previous page. Next select **Printer properties** from the menu which appears. The **Printer Properties** window opens and from this select the **Sharing** tab as shown below.

Now make sure the check box next to **Share this printer** is ticked as shown above. The printer is now available for other computers to detect and share. However, as stated above, other computers cannot detect this printer unless the host computer and the printer are fully up and running and not "sleeping". There is also an opportunity to give a different **Share name** to the printer to make it easy to identify if you have more than one printer on the network.

Detecting a Printer on a Wireless Network

The next task is to make a connection between the other computers and the printer. Make sure the host computer with the printer physically attached is fully up and running. Then from each of the other computers in turn (sometimes known as *workstations* or *network clients*) carry out the following procedure.

Click the Start button and select **Devices and Printers** as shown on page 141. From the top of the **Devices and Printers** window click **Add a printer**, as shown below.

Then select **Add a network, wireless or Bluetooth printer** as shown below and click **Next.**

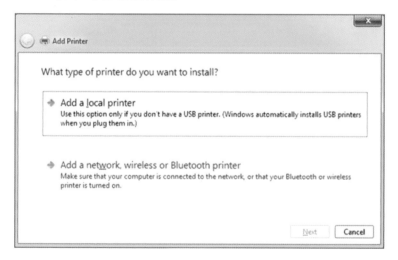

The computer starts searching for available printers on the network and all being well the computer finds the required one, as shown highlighted in blue below. This is a **Brother** printer attached by a cable to the network computer called **HPOFFICE**.

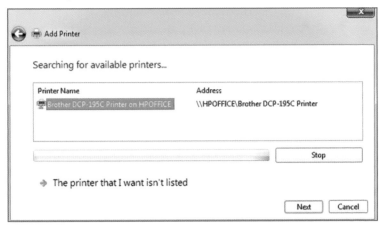

When the required printer is listed click **Next**. You should quickly see the following window, confirming that the printer has been successfully installed with the correct driver software. If Windows cannot find the correct driver software you will need to insert the manufacturer's CD which came with the printer.

After clicking **Next** you are given the option to print a test page to make sure the printer is working correctly.

Using the Internet

Introduction

Microsoft Windows includes Internet Explorer, a *Web browser*. This is a program used for displaying Web pages and navigating between different Web sites. An icon for Internet Explorer (shown on the right) is automatically pinned to the Windows Taskbar by default, as shown below.

Several other companies produce Web browsers in competition with Microsoft's Internet Explorer. Some of these companies felt that Internet Explorer had an unfair advantage, being an integral part of the Windows operating system installed on 90% of the world's computers. As a result Windows now includes a Browser Choice window giving users the chance to install any one of eleven browsers. Internet Explorer remains the most popular Web browser, with Google Chrome and Mozilla Firefox its nearest challengers.

Search Engines

A Web browser such as Internet Explorer uses a program called a *search engine* to find Web pages containing specified information. Google is probably the world's most popular search engine, as discussed shortly. (The Google search engine is not to be confused with the Google Chrome Web browser).

The Windows operating system includes Bing, Microsoft's own search engine, shown below ready to carry out a keyword search for information on, for example, the **peregrine falcon**.

Launching Internet Explorer

Internet Explorer is launched very easily by a single click on its icon, shown on the right, pinned by default to the Windows Taskbar as shown below.

The Internet Explorer opens at the Home Page as shown below.

The Home Page is the first page you see whenever you start Internet Explorer. If you navigate your way to several other Web pages, you can return to the Home Page directly by clicking the Home icon shown on the right. The Home icon is shown in context below on the **Command bar**. A different Web page can be set as your Home Page after clicking the small arrow to the right of the Home icon.

Surfing the Internet

The Internet is a collection of millions of Web pages stored on computers all round the world. These computers, known as *Web servers*, are provided by companies and organisations so that individual users can access information. A Web page usually contains text and pictures but multi-media content such as music, sound and video clips may also appear on a page.

There are various ways you can connect to a Web site on an Internet server computer; then you can move around the pages on the site. Methods of accessing Web pages and sites include:

- Clicking a *link* or *hyperlink* on a Web page. When you pass the cursor over a link, the cursor changes to a hand. A link may be a piece of text or a picture.

- Typing the unique address of a Web site, such as **www.babanibooks.com** into the Address Bar at the top of the Internet Explorer screen.

- Entering *keywords* such as **red squirrel** into a search engine such as Bing or Google.

Clickable Links or Hyperlinks

Click the Internet Explorer icon on the Taskbar at the bottom of the screen, as shown on the right, to open the Home Page as shown on the previous page. (Your own Home Page may be different). If you move the cursor about the screen, you should see the cursor change to a hand when it is over certain pieces of text or pictures. In addition a piece of text may become underlined when the cursor rolls over it. These are the clickable *links* or *hyperlinks* to other Web pages or Web sites. For example, on my Home Page there is a link to a gadgets Web page, as shown underlined below.

> **Smart gadgets and technology** that allow you to go beyond the realms of human limitations

When you click the **Smart gadgets and technology** link shown on the previous page, the site opens up, as shown below.

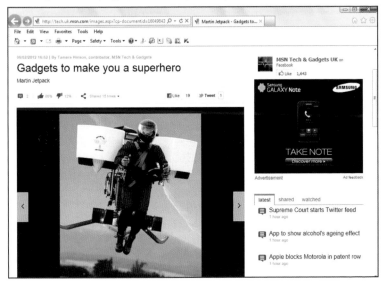

Now you can continue moving around the Internet, clicking any links that interest you. Use the forward and back arrows shown on the left below to move between Web pages already visited.

Returning to the Home Page

As mentioned previously, you can return to your Home Page directly at any time by clicking the Home icon shown on the right and on the Command Bar shown below.

Another Home icon appears at the top right-hand corner of the screen, as shown on the right.

The Stop Icon

Sometimes after clicking a link, the requested page will not open and the computer just appears to freeze. If this happens, the Web site may be out of action, for example while maintenance is carried out. In this case, you may have to abandon the attempt to open the Web page. This is done by clicking the Stop icon, represented by the cross towards the top centre of the Internet Explorer screen, shown on the right and below.

Changing Your Home Page

You can designate any page you like as your Home Page. First use Internet Explorer and the methods described on page 147 to navigate to the Web page you want to use as your Home Page. Then click the arrow on the right of the Home Page icon shown on the right. From the small menu which drops down, select **Add or Change Home Page...**. Now select one of the two options shown below and click **Yes** to change the Home Page. (Web page tabs are discussed later in this chapter.)

Typing in a Web Address

To use this method of navigating to a Web site, you obviously need to obtain the address, perhaps from an advertisement or newspaper article. Exact spelling and punctuation are important. Every Web site has a unique address, such as:

http://www.mycompany.co.uk/

This is entered manually into the Address Bar across the top of the Internet Explorer Web browser, as shown below:

In computing jargon, the address of a Web site is known as a *URL* or *Uniform Resource Locator*. In the above example, the meanings of the parts of the address are as follows:

http:

HyperText Transfer Protocol. This is a set of rules used by Web servers. *ftp* is another protocol used for transferring files across the Internet.

www

This means the site is part of the World Wide Web.

mycompany.co.uk

This part of the Web address is known as the *domain name* and is usually based on the name of the company or organization owning the Web site.

co.uk

This denotes a Web site owned by a UK company. **co** is known as the *domain type*.

Other common Web site domain types include:

biz	Business
com	Company or Commercial organization
eu	European Community
info	Information site or service
me.uk	UK individual
org	Non-profit making organization
gov	Government
net	Internet company

In addition, some Web addresses include the code for a country, such as **fr** and **uk** as in: **http://www.mycompany.co.uk**

If you know the address of a Web site, enter this into the Address Bar at the top of the Web browser as shown below. (In practice you can usually miss out the **http://www.** part of the address. This will be filled in automatically.)

When you press **Enter** your browser should connect to the Web site and display its Home Page on the screen. Then you can start moving about the site using the links within the page as described earlier. Now click the small downward pointing arrowhead, second left of the four icons shown here on the right and below.

A list of recently visited Web addresses is displayed. If you click one of the addresses it will be placed in the Address Bar. If necessary press **Enter** to connect to this new Web site.

Finding Information — the Keyword Search

The *keyword search* is the usual way to find information on the Internet. Suppose you want to find out about the **red squirrel**, for example. Start up Internet Explorer from its icon on the Windows Taskbar, shown on the right.
Now enter **red squirrel** in the Bing search bar as shown below. (As discussed shortly, there are several other search engines, such as Google.)

Now click the **Web Search** button shown on the right above. Bing searches the Internet for any Web pages containing the words **red squirrel**. Then a list of all of the relevant Web sites (over 33 million) is displayed, as shown in the sample below.

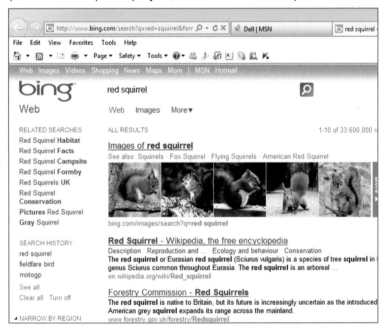

The search results shown below are extracts from Web sites containing the key words **red** and **squirrel**. The underlined headings are clickable links to open the Web sites..

As shown on the right above, millions of results are found. Normally, if you're lucky, you find what you want on the first page. The first page should contain the most relevant results. Click anywhere on the coloured, underlined text links to open up a Web page containing the keywords — **red squirrel** in this example.

When searching for Web pages containing several keywords, the results may include pages which contain the keywords anywhere on the page, even if they are separated and in the wrong order as in "a grey **squirrel** chased by a **Red** Setter". To exclude such unwanted search results, enclose the keywords in speech marks or inverted commas, as shown below. This new search will only list Web sites where the words **red** and **squirrel** appear next to each other and in the correct order.

When the search was repeated with inverted commas as shown, below, the number of search results dropped from over 33,600,000 to 1,380,000.

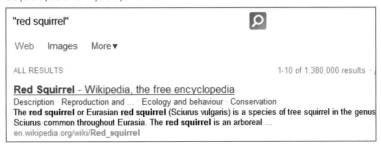

This huge drop in search results occurred because the only Web sites listed now are those where the words **red** and **squirrel** are next to each other on the Web page

Another cause of unwanted search results is the fact that the keywords used in a search may be found in a Web site which is irrelevant to the current search. For example, when searching for information on the red squirrel you are probably only concerned with the small omnivore faced with extinction. You are probably not interested in the Web sites of companies who choose to use **Red Squirrel** as names of their products, as shown below.

Fortunately the most relevant Web sites usually appear at the top of the list of results for the search.

Advertising on Web Pages

When you look at the results of a search you will often see advertisements from companies, usually down the right-hand side of the Web page. These are for products or services which are relevant to the current search. For example, shown below are the results of a search displayed after entering **cruise holidays** into the Bing search bar, as previously described.

Down the right-hand side are clickable links to the Web sites of companies who have paid to advertise on the search results page. So companies selling cruises, for example, are only one click away from individual users searching for cruise information.

Web-based search engines like Bing and Google and the Facebook social networking site are free to the individual user. This is possible because these Internet companies earn their revenue from targeted advertising. (Google is discussed shortly).

Click Through Rate

This is a measure of the success of advertising on Web sites. It is used in the calculation of the fees paid by the advertisers to the owners of the Web sites, such as Microsoft (owners of Bing), Google and Facebook. It is based on the number of times the advertisement is clicked to take an individual user through to the Web site of the company paying for the advertisement.

The Google Search Engine

Google is a highly acclaimed and freely available alternative to the Bing search engine provided with Windows. Google has a reputation for finding relevant results very quickly; the program is so popular that the verb "to Google" is now in common use.

To launch Google, enter **www.google.co.uk** into the Address Bar of Internet Explorer, as shown below.

The Google search screen opens as shown below, ready for you to enter the keywords into the search bar, such as **Red Squirrel,** for example. A forward slash is added automatically.

Click the **Google Search** button to find Web pages containing the keywords. As shown above, the search can focus on various categories such as **News**, **Images** or **Maps**, for example, as shown above. The **I'm Feeling Lucky** button is used when you think Google will find the required page instantly. This opens the page without listing the other results of the search.

Adding a Desktop Icon for Google

Right-click anywhere over the Google screen and select **Create Shortcut** from the menu which appears. Then click the **Yes** button shown below to place an icon on the Windows Desktop.

The Google icon appears on the Desktop as shown on the right. Now you can launch Google by double-clicking the icon on the Windows Desktop.

Launching Google from a Jump List

When you visit Web sites using Internet Explorer, recently visited sites are listed in a Jump List, as shown on the right. This list appears when you right click the Internet Explorer icon on the Taskbar.

If you click the pin icon shown on the right and above right, Google is pinned to the Jump List. You can then launch Google whenever you want to, with just a single click of the Google entry on the Jump List on the Taskbar.

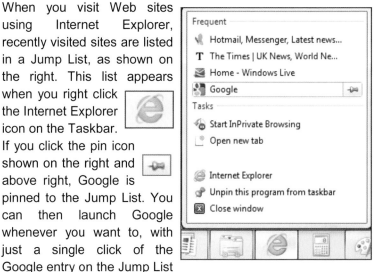

Tabbed Browsing

This feature in later versions of Internet Explorer enables you to open several Web sites in one window. Previous versions of Internet Explorer required you to open a separate window for each Web site. Clicking the tabs makes it easy to switch between Web sites.

In the screen extract below, the Address Bar is shown on the left. To the right of the Address bar are tabs for three Web sites currently open, namely **The RSPB**, **Genealogy...** and **Facebook**.

Clicking any of the tabs, shown again enlarged below, displays the associated Web page on the full screen.

Sometimes you may only see a single Web site tab on your computer instead of several, as shown above. The number of tabs you see depends on the way you open a new Web page. For example, if you type a Web address such as **www.bbc.co.uk** straight into the Address Bar and press **Enter** or **Return**, the new site will be opened, replacing the tab for the previous site. The Address Bar is shown on the left below with the tab for the current Web page (**BBC-Homepage**) on the right.

The next page shows how new tabs can be opened for Web pages so that they appear in a row alongside the existing tabs, such as the **BBC-Homepage** above.

Opening Tabs for Multiple Web Pages

However, if you click the small square shown on the right and on the extreme right below, this will open a new tab, also shown below.

The Address Bar now contains the words **about:Tabs**. Delete the words **about:Tabs** and type a new Web address into the Address Bar. The name of the new Web site will now appear on the new tab, replacing the words **New Tab**, as shown below.

This procedure can be repeated many times so that you have multiple Web sites open simultaneously.

In addition to clicking the small **New Tab** square, shown above there are some other ways to have several Web pages open simultaneously, with their tabs displayed in a row across the top of the screen. These include the following:

* Press the **Ctrl** key while clicking a link on a Web page.

* After typing an address into the Address Bar, (discussed on page 150), hold down the **Alt** key and press the **Enter** key, also known as the **Return** key.

* Click over a link using the *middle* mouse button (if you have one).

* Right-click over a link and select **Open in New Tab** from the drop-down menu.

With the tabs of several Web pages displayed across the top of the screen you can quickly move between Web pages by clicking the tabs, displaying them each in turn on the full screen.

Displaying Web Pages Using Quick Tabs

If you have opened a lot of Web pages, the tabs don't show what each page looks like. The **Quick Tabs** feature in Windows displays a grid of miniature versions of each Web page, often referred to as "thumbnails".

To make sure the **Quick Tabs** feature is switched on in Internet Explorer, select **Tools** from the Menu Bar as shown below.

Then from the drop-down menu, select **Internet Options** and make sure the **General** tab is selected.. From the **Tabs** section of the **Internet Options** menu which appears, select **Settings**, as shown below.

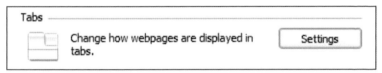

The **Tabbed Browsing Settings** window opens, as shown in the extract below.

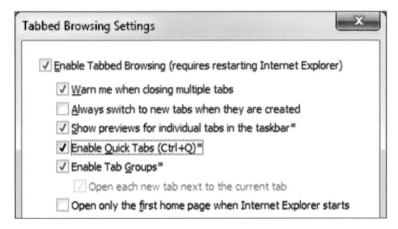

In the **Tabbed Browsing Settings** window, make sure there is a tick in the check box next to **Enable Quick Tabs (Ctrl+Q)**, as shown near the bottom of the previous page. To complete the process you need to restart Internet Explorer.

The **Quick Tabs** are displayed as shown below when you hold down **Ctrl** and press **Q**. Alternatively, click **View** on the Menu Bar and then select **Quick tabs**, as shown below.

If the words **Quick tabs** appear greyed out on the **View** menu, check that **Enable Quick Tabs** is switched on in the **Tabbed Browsing Settings** window, as shown on the previous page. The **Quick Tabs** window opens as shown below, enabling you to get a quick view of each Web page.

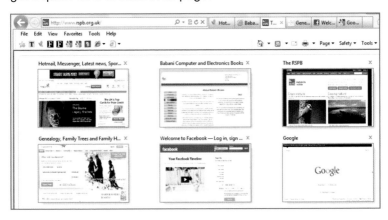

A thumbnail can be clicked to view the page on the full screen or the page can be closed by clicking a cross in the top right corner.

Revisiting Web Sites

The History and Favorites features allow you to return to Web sites which you have visited days or weeks previously.

History

The History feature keeps, for a specified time, a list of all of the Web sites you've visited. To open History, click **View**, **Explorer bars** and make sure **History** is ticked. A single click will relaunch any of the previously visited Web sites, such as **www.ancestry.co.uk** listed below. The History list can be arranged in various ways such as alphabetical or by date, after clicking the small arrow on the right of **View By Date**.

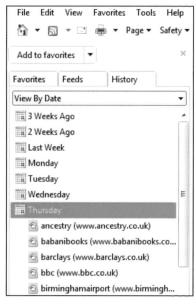

To alter the settings of the History feature, from the Internet Explorer Menu bar, select **Tools** and **Internet options**. Make sure the **General** tab is selected in the Internet Options window. From the **Browsing history** section click the **Settings** button. This opens the **Temporary Internet Files and History Settings** window. The **History** section at the bottom allows you to specify the number of days you wish to keep Web pages in the list, as shown below.

History

Specify how many days Internet Explorer should save the list of websites you have visited.

Days to keep pages in history: 20

Favorites

This feature allows you to "bookmark" sites that you may want to look at in the future. While the required Web site is open on the screen, click **Favorites** from the Internet Explorer Menu Bar and then click **Add to favorites**. You can either accept the name suggested in the **Add a Favorite** window shown below or type in your preferred name and then click the **Add** button.

To display your list of favourites at any time, click **Favorites** on the Internet Explorer Menu Bar. Click any of the entries in the list as shown on the right to relaunch the associated Web page.

The **Organize favorites...** option shown on the right allows you to rename and delete favourites and categorize them into new folders. To arrange the list of favourites in alphabetical order, right-click over the list and click **Sort by name**.

The Favorites and History features can also be accessed from their tabs by clicking the star icon in the top right-hand corner of the screen as shown on the right in the middle.

Cached Web Pages

Sometimes when you click a link to open a Web page, the computer just seems to hang, with just a revolving circle at the cursor position. The Web page may not be available because it is being worked on or because too many people are trying to access it. Search Engines such as Google *crawl* the Web pages on the Internet and make their own snapshot copies called *cached* Web pages. The pages in the cache may not be the same as the latest ones on the actual Web site, if the Web site has been updated since the last crawl by the search engine.

If a cached copy of a Web page is available, two arrows appear when you hover the cursor over the right of the entry in the list of search results, as shown below. A small view of the Web page appears as shown on the right below.

Click the word **Cached** to view the full size Web page. The cached Web page opens as shown below. The words used in the keyword search, such as **Barn** and **Owl**, are highlighted.

Barn Owl

From Wikipedia, the free encyclopedia

The **Barn Owl** (*Tyto alba*) is the most widely distributed species of **owl**, and one of the most widespread of all birds. It is als in the **barn-owl** family Tytonidae. These form one of two main lineages of living owls, the other being the typical owls (Strigid desert regions, Asia north of the Alpide belt, most of Indonesia, and the Pacific islands.[1]

It is known by many other names, which may refer to the appearance, call, habitat or the eerie, silent flight: White **Owl**, Silver **Owl**, Cave **Owl**, Stone **Owl**, Monkey-faced **Owl**, Hissing **Owl**, Hobgoblin or Hobby **Owl**, Dobby **Owl**, White Breasted **Owl**, G Delicate **Owl**. "Golden **Owl**" might also refer to the related Golden Masked **Owl** (*T. aurantia*). "Hissing **Owl**" and, particularly The latter name, however, more correctly applies to a different group of birds, the screech-owls in the genus *Megascops*. The

The cached page may be useful as a backup when the latest version of a Web page is not available, for whatever reason.

Cached Web pages produced by the Bing search engine can be displayed using essentially the same method as used for Google.

Temporary Internet Files

When you visit a Web site for the first time, copies of the Web pages are saved on your computer's hard disc drive. Next time you click to visit the Web site, the Web browser retrieves the saved Web pages from your hard disc drive, not the ones stored on the Internet server. Retrieving pages from your local hard disc drive is quicker than copying the originals from server. You can change the way Internet Explorer checks for stored Web pages after clicking **Tools**, **Internet Options** and **Browser History** as shown below. Deleting temporary files is discussed later.

Temporary Internet Files

Internet Explorer stores copies of webpages, images, and media for faster viewing later.

Check for newer versions of stored pages:

⦾ Every time I visit the webpage

⦾ Every time I start Internet Explorer

◉ Automatically

⦾ Never

Cookies

These are small text files which are automatically stored on your computer when you browse the Internet. They record your browsing habits and interests which may be used for marketing purposes by commercial Web sites. Cookies may be used to enhance your browsing experience — for example to assist with online shopping. To delete cookies, select **Tools**, **Internet options**, and select the **General** tab. Under **Browsing History** click **Delete**. Make sure **Cookies** is ticked and click the **Delete** button. However, deleting cookies may have an adverse affect on the smooth running of some Web sites. You can also block cookies after selecting **Internet options**, clicking the **Privacy tab** and then **Advanced**.

Alternative Web Browsers

This chapter has been based on Microsoft Internet Explorer, currently the most popular Web browser. However, after complaints from other browser producers, Microsoft has agreed to offer a choice of alternative browsers. These can be downloaded from a *Browser Choice* window as shown below.

The Browser Choice is displayed if you are currently using Internet Explorer as your browser and the **Automatic Updates** setting is turned on in Windows Update. Before the Browser Choice window opens, a note appears explaining the choice of browsers. Click **OK** to open the Browser Choice window as shown below. The Browser Choice window can also be launched by clicking its icon on the Windows Desktop as shown on the right.

Five popular browsers appear on the window initially and six more can be seen by dragging the horizontal scroll bar. A description of each browser is displayed by clicking **Tell me more**, as shown above. Click **Install** and **Run** to set up one of the above Web browsers on your computer.

If Internet Explorer is not selected, its icon (shown on the right) is unpinned from the Taskbar. Internet Explorer will still be available from the Start/All Programs menu and its icon can be pinned back on the Taskbar.

11

Internet Activities

Introduction

Previous chapters discussed the setting up of an Internet Connection and the methods used to find Web pages containing the information you require. This chapter describes some of the Web sites which we find particularly useful ourselves. In this context, the terms Web site and Web page are interchangeable, since a Web site is simply one or more Web pages or documents.

It may be helpful at this point to recap on the methods by which you can arrive at a particular Web site, as discussed in more detail in the previous chapter.

- Typing the unique address or URL of a Web site, such as **www.babanibooks.com** into the Address Bar.

- Entering *keywords* such as **barn owl** into a search engine such as Bing or Google.

- Clicking a *link* or *hyperlink* on a Web page.

- Selecting a Web site from the list of *Favorites* which you have created. (<u>Favorites</u> is the American spelling used in the software).

- Selecting a Web site from the *History* list which is automatically created by Internet Explorer.

- Selecting a Web site from a *Jump List* displayed when you right click over the Internet Explorer icon, as described on page 87.

As shown on the next page, the Address Bar in Internet Explorer also keeps a list of recently visited Web sites.

Click the small downward pointing arrow on the left of the three icons shown here on the right of the Address Bar. A drop-down list of recently visited Web sites appears, as shown below.

Click any of the addresses in the list to return to that Web site.

Searching from the Address Bar

This option allows you to use the Address Bar for keyword searches in addition to entering Web site addresses. To switch this option on, select **Tools**, **Internet options** and from the **Search** section, shown below, click the **Settings** button.

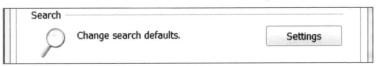

Click to place a tick in the check box next to **Search in the address bar**, as shown below.

> ☐ Prevent programs from suggesting changes to my default search provider
> ☑ Search in the address bar
>
> Find more search providers...
> Learn more about search provider preferences

Now click the **Close** button and a magnifying glass appears in the Address Bar as shown on the right. Type the keywords into the Address Bar and click the magnifying glass icon to carry out a search from the Address Bar instead of from the Search Bar.

Searching With Google

This has to be one of the most popular Internet activities. We invariably find what we want to know. No matter how obscure the subject, people have usually put copious amounts of information on the World Wide Web for all to see. Scientific and Medical information is provided by experts in their field which you can view within seconds without paying a penny, apart from the cost of your Internet service. If you want to know how to tackle a particular tricky DIY task, you'll almost certainly find several videos telling you how to it. If your interested in ornithology, enter a species such as   **Barn Owl** into a search engine such as Google or Bing as shown below. After clicking the **Search** button (the magnifying glass icon on the right below) or pressing Enter, 1,250,000 Web sites are listed in a fraction of a second.

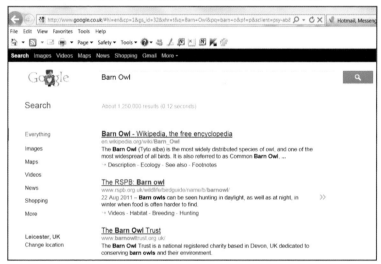

Near the top of the list is the RSPB Web site. The two arrows to the right of the RSPB result shown above lead to the *cached* copies of the Web page, as described in the last chapter on page 164. If you click the link **The RSPB: Barn owl** shown above, the Web site opens as shown on the next page.

Links to Multi-media Clips

This excellent Web site gives comprehensive details about each bird including their favourite habitats, food and estimated numbers. The Web site also includes clickable links

to multi-media clips, such as a sample of a bird's call or song and a video showing the bird in flight. Alphabetical buttons at the top right of the main screen allow you to find information about an enormous range of other birds, after clicking on the species.

This Web site demonstrates the power of the Internet to deliver up-to-date multi-media information which can be searched and displayed rapidly — unlike a book or a wall chart, for example.

Searching Google Categories

Google allows you to concentrate a search on various categories such as **Images**, **Videos**, **Maps** and **News** from the Google bar shown below.

If you select **Images** and then enter **Barn Owl**, for example, in the Google Search Bar, an array of thumbnail images appears.

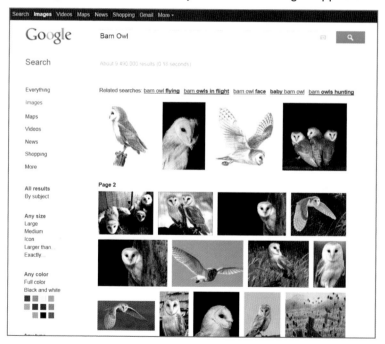

Click any of the thumbnails above to display a larger version of the image.

Google Earth and Street View

This program is from the same company as the Google search engine and the Google Chrome Web browser. Google also produce their own e-mail software known as Gmail. Google Earth provides high quality maps based on satellite images and aerial photographs of the world with the ability to search for a particular location. This includes zooming in to get a close-up view. The most extreme zoom leads to Google Street View which gives 3-D images of a neighbourhood including panoramic views of houses, gardens and any people and vehicles present at the time the area was photographed.

Google Earth is free and you can download a copy to your computer after entering Google Earth into the Google search engine as shown below.

Click the link **Google Earth** shown above and then follow the instructions on the screen. The PC version is suitable for

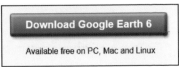

users of Windows XP, Vista and Windows 7. After you have finished the installation, an icon for Google Earth appears on your Windows Desktop, as shown on the right. Double-click this icon to launch Google Earth at any time.

Google Earth opens showing an image of the entire globe. In the top left-hand corner there is a search bar to enter the name of a place you want to look at. When you click the magnifying glass

search icon or press the Enter key, Google Earth descends from the global image and "flies to" the location you have chosen.

Buttons on the right of the screen allow you to zoom in on an area or move in any direction. You can also hold down the left mouse button and drag the cursor to scroll the map. If you zoom in as far as possible, Google Earth opens in *Street View*, as shown below. Street View is also available in Google Maps.

Shopping Online

We have been shopping online and carrying out financial transactions such as banking and paying bills for many years. Obviously there is a concern about security when you enter your account details online but so far we have never lost a penny. One of the first and most successful Internet companies is Amazon, which started in America in 1995 as an online bookstore. Since then it has diversified into a global online retailer of a wide range of goods, especially electronics.

Online retailers like Amazon have several advantages:

- You can view the products and order them from the comfort of your own home without travelling to shops.
- Comprehensive details and specifications of products are given online, which you can digest at leisure, unlike shopping in the hustle and bustle of the High Street.
- Many items may be reviewed online by other customers, giving you unbiased opinions rather than those of sales staff in a shop who may be trying to earn commission.
- It's easier to visit various online retailers to compare prices rather than physically visiting High Street shops.
- The online retailer can despatch goods from a central warehouse without maintaining an expensive High Street presence. So online goods should be cheaper.
- If you are a repeat customer with Amazon, your details are remembered so an item can be purchased with literally one click of the left-hand mouse button.
- In the case of Amazon, goods may be received within a day of placing the order and delivery may be free.
- An online bookseller like Amazon can have millions of books in stock, unlike the smaller High street retailer who may have to order a book from their distributor.

Log on to Amazon by entering their address into the your Web bowser such as Internet Explorer.

The Amazon Web page opens showing the range of departments down the left-hand side. As well as books, the range of goods now includes clothes, electronics, hobbies, grocery and DIY.

Amazon has enjoyed considerable success with its Kindle, a hand-held electronic device used for downloading and reading books from the Internet and known as an *e-book reader*. The image of a Kindle shown above is a clickable link to another page on the Amazon Web site, as shown on the next page.

On the left of the screen shown above is a link to a **Quick Tour**, a video describing the product. In the centre are some technical details. A search bar at the top allows you to look for specific products or you can use the clickable links to browse through different departments. If you want to buy an item you would click **Add to Basket** shown on the right before proceeding to the checkout to complete your personal details such as name, address and bank  details, completing the purchase and choosing a delivery option. New customers create a new account with their e-mail address and password. Existing customers may need to sign in with their stored e-mail address and password. Then they can click **Buy now with 1-Click** and the transaction is completed and delivery arranged with no further input from the customer.

Online Newspapers

Many national and local newspapers can now be read online. The Internet version of a newspaper can be found with a simple search in Bing or Google, for example, as shown below.

After clicking the newspaper's link in the results list, you may see the entire paper straightaway. Many of the online tabloids and local papers are free. Alternatively you may need to sign up as a subscriber with your e-mail address and password. For example, you might need to pay around £2 a week for one of the heavyweight newspapers, obviously much cheaper and more convenient than buying the traditional edition printed on paper.

The online version of a newspaper can show breaking news throughout the day and there is no paper to recycle.

Tracing Your Family History

Finding out about your ancestors used to be a very time-consuming job — visiting churchyards and searching through old parish records and county archives. Or you could pay a professional genealogist to carry out the work. The Internet has greatly simplified the task of tracing your forebears since millions of records have been made available on the Internet. Nowadays records can be retrieved with a search engine like Google or Bing, or by using dedicated genealogy Web sites.

Genealogy online is now extremely popular and as a result there are many specialist Web sites such as **findmypast.co.uk**, **Ancestry.co.uk** and **FreeBMD**. These genealogy Web sites allow you to access millions of records from the Civil Registrations of births, marriages and deaths and the National Censuses. The Web sites have built-in facilities to search for people. Shown below is a search using findmypast.co.uk to find a marriage, after entering the person's name and approximate year of the marriage.

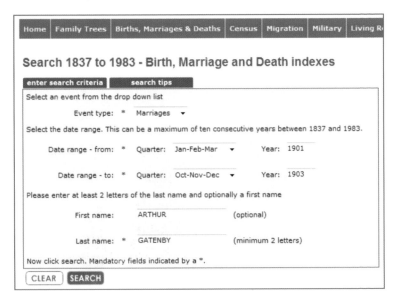

The results are presented in normal text on the computer screen but you can also view and print a copy of the original document, which may have been handwritten or produced on a manual typewriter, as shown below.

Web sites like findmypast.co.uk also include options to order copies of official Birth, Marriage and Death Certificates, to be delivered within a few days by the traditional post.

Ancestry.co.uk has one of the largest collections of family records and has sponsored the transcribing of millions of handwritten Birth, Marriage and Death records into a format searchable by computer. The ancestry.co.uk Web site also has facilities to enable you to create, save and print your family tree.

Another major source of family records is the U.K. National Censuses available every 10 years from 1841 to 1911. These give the name, sex, age and occupation, etc., of everyone living in a household on the night of the census, as shown below.

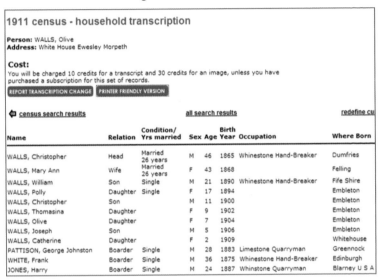

1911 census - household transcription

Person: WALLS, Olive
Address: White House Ewesley Morpeth

Cost:
You will be charged 10 credits for a transcript and 30 credits for an image, unless you have purchased a subscription for this set of records.

REPORT TRANSCRIPTION CHANGE   PRINTER FRIENDLY VERSION

◀ census search results   all search results   redefine cu

Name	Relation	Condition/ Yrs married	Sex	Age	Birth Year	Occupation	Where Born
WALLS, Christopher	Head	Married 26 years	M	46	1865	Whinestone Hand-Breaker	Dumfries
WALLS, Mary Ann	Wife	Married 26 years	F	43	1868		Felling
WALLS, William	Son	Single	M	21	1890	Whinestone Hand-Breaker	Fife Shire
WALLS, Polly	Daughter	Single	F	17	1894		Embleton
WALLS, Christopher	Son		M	11	1900		Embleton
WALLS, Thomasina	Daughter		F	9	1902		Embleton
WALLS, Olive	Daughter		F	7	1904		Embleton
WALLS, Joseph	Son		M	5	1906		Embleton
WALLS, Catherine	Daughter		F	2			Whitehouse
PATTISON, George Johnston	Boarder	Single	M	28	1883	Limestone Quarryman	Greennock
WHITE, Frank	Boarder	Single	M	36	1875	Whinestone Hand-Breaker	Edinburgh
JONES, Harry	Boarder	Single	M	24	1887	Whinstone Quarryman	Blarney U S A

As shown below, ancestry.co.uk, provides records from the National Censuses, the Births, Marriages and Deaths Registers, Military Records from World Wars I and II, and immigration, ships' passenger lists and parish and criminal records.

Our records hold the key to your family history...

Census records
Censuses are perhaps the most important genealogy records — and we have the most complete online collection. Move back through the generations with details such as addresses, ages and occupations

Birth, marriage & death indexes
Build a timeline of your ancestors' lives with our complete birth, marriage and death indexes from 1837 to 2005. Discover where and when each event happened, then order full certificates for even more

Military records
Trace the war heroes in your family with millions of military records. We have the largest online collection of World War I records, plus comprehensive collections for World War II and many earlier conflicts

Plus much more!
Discover your ancestors' stones and build your family tree with immigration records, parish records, criminal records, the National Probate Calendar and over 6 billion other records from all over the world!

More detailed coverage of Ancestry is given in our book BP 720 How to Trace Your Ancestors Using a Computer for the Older Generation.

Arranging a Holiday

You can make all your holiday arrangements online without having to leave home to visit a travel agent. Prices on the Internet are usually cheaper than traditional methods of booking and you can compare prices easily and get last minute deals.

Finding Out About a Destination

A quick search with Google or Bing will provide lots of useful information about a place you are thinking of visiting.

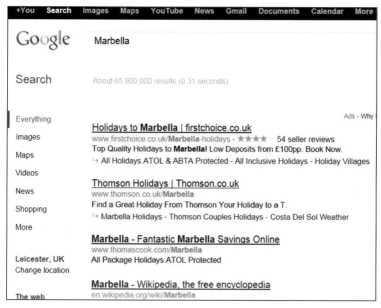

The search results will include links to the main travel companies offering holidays to the area. There will also be official Web sites giving details of resorts and tourist attractions. The link to the free online encyclopedia Wikipedia will also give a lot of useful background information about the history of a place. Entering something like **weather Tenerife** into your search engine such as Google should produce current weather details, weekly or longer forecasts and year round averages, as shown overleaf.

Weather for **Tenerife, Spain**

12°C | °F

Scattered Clouds
Wind: NW at 10 mph
Humidity: 88%

	Fri	Sat	Sun	Mon
	16° 12°	15° 12°	15° 11°	16° 12°

Detailed forecast: The Weather Channel - Weather Underground - AccuWeather

Webcams

Many hotels and resorts have set up *webcams* to take pictures which are updated regularly. For example, to get views of Nice, France enter something like **webcam Nice** into a search engine.

Then click the links in the list of search results to view the various webcams as shown in the Nice example below.

Booking a Hotel

After carrying out a search for a destination, there will be lots of links to firms offering deals including hotels and flights, including special last minute

Cheap Hotels in Marbella
www.laterooms.com/**Marbella**-Hotels
laterooms.com is rated ★ ★ ★ ★ ⋆
Cheap 4" Hotels in **Marbella**.
With Up to 50% Off! Book Online.

offers. You may find that a link to the TripAdvisor Web site appears after a search for a hotel. For each hotel there should be a large number of reviews by previous guests.

The hotel Web site normally includes the room prices. There may be sample menus and views of the different types of room. Some hotels include a virtual tour or video of all of the facilities of the hotel including the restaurant, bars and swimming pool.

Search Hotels

Destination/hotel name:
Edinburgh

Check-in date
[ ] Day ⏷ Month ⏷

Check-out date
[ ] Day ⏷ Month ⏷

☐ I don't have specific dates yet

Rooms	1 ⏷
Adults	2 ⏷
Children	0 ⏷

Search

The hotel Web site allows you to check room availability for your dates, as shown on the right. Then you can proceed to make an online booking. You may be required to pay straightaway or at the end of your stay. **A credit card gives greater protection for your payment than a debit card.**

Rooms & Suites

Hotel Cipriani offers 79 beautifully decorated suites and rooms, with magnificent views over the open lagoon and the gardens. **Palazzo Vendramin** is a 15th-century residence linked to the Hotel Cipriani through an ancient courtyard and a passageway lined with flowers. It houses 16 suites and rooms with sweeping vistas over the gardens and across to St Mark's Square.

Rooms & Suites - Hotel Cipriani

The 79 delightful suites and rooms of the Hotel Cipriani offer breathtaking views over the open lagoon and the Casanova gardens.

Read more »

Rooms & Suites - Palazzo Vendramin

Palazzo Vendramin, a charming, 15th-century residence linked to the Hotel Cipriani through a pretty, ancient courtyard, is home to 16 rooms and suites with glorious views towards St Mark's Square.

Read more »

Arranging Flights Online

You'll probably know which airport you'd like to use for your trip. Enter the airport name into a search engine like Google. The airport site will have links to their flight destinations and time-tables. From these you can find out if there are any flights to your chosen destination. If suitable flights are available, you can enter your required dates and obtain prices.

Before making an online booking to purchase tickets, you may be able to compare prices with other airlines, perhaps operating out of different airports. Where we live in Derbyshire people regularly fly from Birmingham, Manchester, Gatwick, Heathrow and East Midlands. The Internet makes it easy to compare prices and match your requirements such as destinations, dates and times.

✈ Flights only   ✈🏨 Flights + Hotels

Destination
New Zealand ▾

Airport
Christchurch (CHC) ▾

Date Leaving   Date Returning
Wed 29/02/2012   Wed 07/03/2012

Adults (18+)   Children (2-17)
1 ▾   0 ▾

Infants (under 2)
0 ▾

☐ Only Direct Flights   ☐ One Way Only

Search →

Book flights and holidays here or alternatively call Airport Direct Travel on 0800 655 6470.

Several Web sites are designed to help you to find cheap flights and compare prices. You could type one of the following into the Address Bar of your Web browser such as Internet Explorer:

www.cheapflights.co.uk   www.travelsupermarket.com

Alternatively enter the keywords **cheap flights** into your search engine and follow the links in the results to the various Web sites.

Some airlines now allow you to *check in* online. This can save a lot of queuing at the airport, answering questions and waiting for your boarding pass to be printed. Instead you print your boarding pass at home on your own computer, together with confirmation documents that act as your tickets. You may also be able to choose where you sit on the plane (for an additional charge).

Tracking Flights in Real Time

You can use your computer to check flights in real time, even if the planes are hundreds or thousands of miles away. This might be useful if you were waiting for a friend or relative to arrive. Enter the keywords **flight tracking** into your search engine.

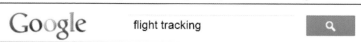

Numerous links to flight tracking Web sites are produced, including **flightradar24.com**. This site is free to use and can be launched by entering the following into your Address Bar:

www.flightradar24.com

If you know the flight number of an aircraft, such as **UAE17** for example, select the **Planes** tab and scroll down to the flight listing. Then click **Show on map** to see the plane's position.

The map shows that flight **UAE17** (highlighted in red) is currently over the Netherlands. The left-hand panel shows it is a United Arab Emirates Airbus A380 travelling from Dubai to Manchester at an altitude of 40000ft and a speed of 481mph.

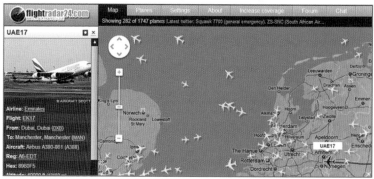

To see the details of planes currently flying overhead in your area, scroll the map to show your area and click on the icons for each of the planes in turn. Buttons on the left allow you to zoom in and out and move in any direction.

Buying and Selling on eBay

If you are thinking of downsizing or simply want to get rid of some "clutter", *eBay* allows you to offer your items to a nationwide or worldwide audience of millions of potential customers. The range of goods offered for sale on eBay is enormous, from jewellery, antiques, porcelain and collectable items through to motor vehicles and even real aircraft. Open the Web site by entering the following into the Address Bar of your Web browser.

As shown below, each item is listed with a photograph and a brief description.

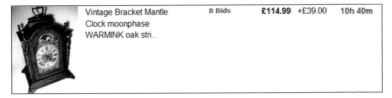

A time limit for the sale, usually several days, is set by the seller and eBay displays a running total of the number of bids, the highest bid received so far (**£114.99** in the example above) and the amount of time left for bidding. The cost of posting (e.g. **£39.00** above) is also shown. At the end of the time allowed, the item is sold to the highest bidder who then pays the seller before the seller arranges delivery by normal post. Obviously in the case of very large items like cars or furniture, for example, buyer and seller must liaise to make arrangements for collection.

PayPal is a security system used by eBay to protect the purchaser's payment against the goods not being delivered and also ensures that the seller receives their payment instantly. A feature called **Meet the seller** allows you to check the seller's record, including the number of transactions made and a rating based on the amount of positive feedback from other users.

Useful Web Sites

There are many Web sites containing useful information especially for older people. The following Web addresses can be typed straight in after clicking in the Address Bar. You don't need to enter **http://** and in most cases **www.** is not needed either as these are added automatically. Most of the Web sites give advice and information on topics such as health, finance, shopping and travel for the over 50s.

www.ageuk.org.uk Support for older people.

www.agepartnership.co.uk Equity release specialists.

www.aarp.org Discounts, magazine and online information.

www.cennet.co.uk Holidays for the over 50s.

www.direct.gov.uk Guide to government services.

www.dwp.gov.uk Advice on benefits, work and pensions.

www.facebook.com Rekindle old friendships and make contact with people having similar interests to yourself.

www.fiftyplus.co.uk Fashion catalogue for people over 50.

www.friendsreunited.com Catch up with old school friends.

www.digitalunite.com Digital Unite (DU) – computer training for the over 50s.

www.kelkoo.co.uk Price checks on Internet goods for sale.

www.laterlife.com Promotes a fuller life for the over 50s.

www.neighbourhoodwatch.net Promotes home security.

www.nhsdirect.nhs.uk Advice and help with illness.

www.opin.org.uk Older People's Information Network.

www.overfiftiesfriends.co.uk Senior social networking.

www.rias.co.uk Insurance for over 50s.

www.saga.co.uk Wide range of services for older people.

www.seniority.co.uk Internet community for over 50s.

www.seniorsnetwork.co.uk News and information.

www.ship-ltd.org Release capital tied up in your home.

www.silversurfers.net Provides links to an enormous range of Web sites relevant to over 50s in particular.

www.sixtyplussurfers.co.uk Online magazine for over 60s.

www.theoldie.co.uk A witty magazine for *all* ages.

www.thewillsite.co.uk Help in making your own will.

www.thisismoney.co.uk Guide to savings and loans.

www.twitter.com Send and receive text messages up to140 characters long.

www.uswitch.com Look for cheapest gas, electricity and telephone, etc.

The next chapter looks at Web sites designed to help people to share news and information with friends, family and acquaintances, the phenomenon known as *social networking*.

Social Networking and Communication

Introduction

Social networking is an Internet phenomenon that has developed in the last few years and now involves hundreds of millions of people around the world. Social networking Web sites allow people to exchange news, information and photographs. Well-known sites such as Facebook are free to use and make their money from advertising. This chapter also looks at *electronic mail*, one of the first methods of online communication. In a similar context, free world-wide telephone calls using the *Skype* Internet service were discussed on page 11. The following Internet services are covered in this chapter:

Facebook

Users create or renew friendships online to exchange news, photographs and detailed biographical information.

Twitter

Members post small text messages or *tweets* about their current activities. Other people (*followers*) can read and reply to the tweets of anyone they choose to follow.

Blogging

Members construct a *blog (*or *Weblog*), an online diary or journal, which others can read and respond to.

Electronic Mail or E-mail

Users send longer messages, including documents and pictures, to one or more people via their e-mail addresses.

The Facebook Social Network

This is probably the most popular social networking site, with over 800 million users. Although originally started by college students in America, it is now used by people of all ages; Facebook is becoming increasingly popular with older people especially if they have children and grandchildren on the other side of the world. Businesses and celebrities also use Facebook for promotional purposes, enabling them to reach a very large audience with their latest news and information.

Facebook Friends

Facebook is based around the concept of having lots of *friends*. These may include close personal friends and family but may also include people you have never met in the real world. Some people have thousands of "friends" on Facebook.

These virtual friends on Facebook are people with whom you have agreed to share information across the Internet. Facebook identifies people who you might want to invite to be your friends, perhaps because they are in the list of contacts in your e-mail address book and are already members of Facebook. When you join Facebook you can enter a personal profile giving details of your education, employment and interests, etc. This information allows Facebook to suggest people who you might want to invite to be a friend. They can either accept or decline this invitation.

Confidentiality and Security

Facebook provides a platform for you to post on the Internet a great deal of personal and biographical information. The Internet enables this information to be viewed by a potential audience of millions of people. Facebook has *privacy settings* to allow you to restrict the viewing of certain types of information to specific groups of people. It's advisable not to put confidential information on Facebook unless you are thoroughly conversant with the privacy settings. You are also advised not to accept complete strangers as Facebook friends or arrange to meet up with them.

Joining Facebook

Signing up to Facebook just requires you to be at least 13 years of age, with a computer connected to the Internet and a valid e-mail address. The sign up screen appears after you enter **www.facebook.com** into the address bar of your Web browser.

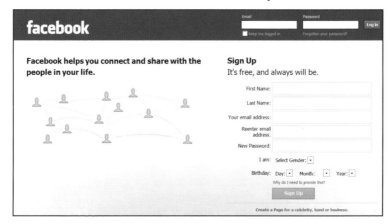

From your e-mail address, Facebook checks your list of e-mail contacts and produces a list of potential friends who are already on Facebook. You can then invite them to be your Facebook friends. Any of your e-mail contacts who are not members of Facebook may be sent an invitation to join the social network.

Your Facebook Profile or Timeline

You are then asked to start entering your *Profile* information, also called your *Timeline*. The profile or timeline contains details such as your education, employment history, address and hobbies and interests, address and contact details

You can also add a profile picture, allowing friends to identify you after a search on Facebook, which may have produced a lot of people with the same name as you. If you have a suitable profile picture stored on your computer it can be uploaded to Facebook, after clicking **Upload a photo**, shown below. Otherwise, if you have a *webcam* on your computer, you can take a picture and upload it directly to Facebook using **Take a photo** shown below.

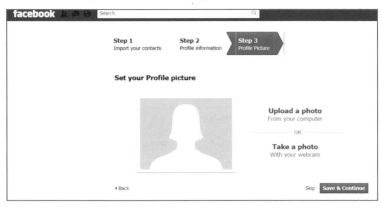

You don't have to fill in every part of your profile or timeline during the sign up process — you can return to edit it later.

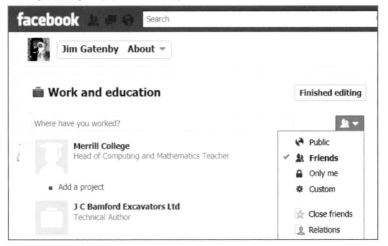

At the right of some pieces of the information is the *inline audience selector* icon shown on the right. Click this icon to open the menu shown above. This allows you to  select the audience for the item of information, e.g. **Public**, **Friends** and **Only me**, etc.

Communicating With Others Via Your Wall

You can type text and add photos in the **Status** box shown on the right and **Post** updates to a "noticeboard" known as your **Wall**. Other people can view your Wall according to the privacy settings such as **Friends** or **Close friends** on the menu shown on the right.

You may also be interested in BP 734 Keeping in Touch Using Social Networking for the Older Generation that will be published later this year.

Tweeting With Twitter

Twitter is another very popular social network with over 200 million users worldwide. Although there are some similarities with Facebook, Twitter is also different in many ways.

What is a Tweet?

One of the main features of Twitter is that messages or *tweets* can be no more than 140 characters long. This makes Twitter suitable for brief text messages like SMS phone texts. As well as PC and Apple computers, Twitter can also be used on the latest smartphones such as the iPhone and the Blackberry.

Whereas e-mail messages are sent to the unique e-mail addresses of known contacts, tweets can be read by very large numbers of people who may be complete strangers to the tweeter. Twitter is based on the idea that users will want to follow the regular pronouncements of other people such as friends, family, celebrities, politicians, reporters or companies and other organisations.

Followers on Twitter

Regular tweeters may post messages several times a day, such as the actor and writer Stephen Fry, who has millions of *followers*. Some users of Twitter will be followers who only read other people's tweets, rather than posting their own. You need to be sufficiently well-known for lots of other people to want to read what you have to say in your tweets, or find ways of encouraging people to become your followers.

You can choose to follow anyone you like on Twitter, but you can't choose who follows you. You can read all the tweets of the people you follow and send a reply if you wish. On Facebook, although some information such as photos and educational details are available for all to see, interaction is usually between people who have agreed to be Facebook "friends". Facebook has privacy settings to control who can see what information.

Hashtags

A hashtag is a word or phrase, etc., preceded by the hash sign (#) and placed in a tweet, e.g. **#BBCQT**. (BBC Question Time in this case). Clicking on a hashtag which appears in a tweet allows you to read all the tweets on that particular topic. You can also find all the relevant tweets by entering the hashtag in the search bar at the top of the Twitter screen as shown below.

Hashtags allow anyone on Twitter to participate in online forums on current news issues or television programs, for example

Twitter in Use

Whereas Facebook relies heavily on detailed personal profiles to bring together people sharing similar backgrounds and interests, Twitter only accepts about a paragraph of biographical information, as shown below under findmypast.co.uk.

Many companies, such as the family history Web site, findmypast.co.uk, include a link to Twitter on their main Web site. Clicking this link opens the Twitter Home page of findmypast.co.uk as shown below.

The latest tweets from **findmypast.co.uk** are displayed down the right-hand side of the screen as shown in the example below.

When you roll the cursor over a tweet, the whole tweet is highlighted in blue as shown above. An extra line of blue text appears along the bottom of the tweet, starting with the time or date the tweet was sent. As you can see above, there are links enabling you to **Reply** to a tweet or to **Retweet**, which means to forward a tweet to your followers. There is also a **Favorites** folder in which to place tweets that you might want to look at in the future.

Shown above is the top of the Twitter page for **findmypast.co.uk**, also shown on page 195. This includes brief details of the company and a link to their Web site. The **Follow** button on the upper right allows you to become a follower of **findmypast.co.uk**. When you are a follower of a person or organisation on Twitter, their tweets appear on the timeline or list of tweets on your Twitter Home page. The figures show total numbers of tweets, the number of people or organisations that **findmypast.co.uk** is following and the number of followers of **findmypast.co.**uk. The **Messages** feature in Twitter allows you to send a Direct, private message to one of your followers. A normal tweet appears on the timeline of all your followers.

Signing up for Twitter

Log on to the Twitter Web site by entering the following in the Address Bar of your Web browser, such as Internet Explorer:

www.twitter.com

Fill in the box, shown on the right, including a valid e-mail address and a password. Then click **Sign up for Twitter**, as shown on the right. Your username, **@samueljohnson** for example, and Twitter account are then created. Then the Twitter Teacher gets you

started by providing a list of people for you to follow. When you click the **Follow** button against a person's name and photo, as shown below, their messages appear on your tweet page.

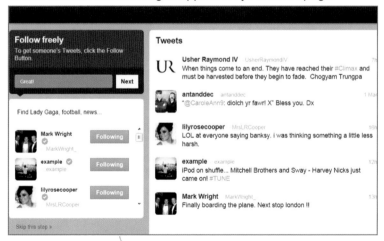

You can also search your e-mail address list for people to follow on Twitter. An image of yourself can be added with a short text profile. An e-mail is sent to you by Twitter and you click on a link for confirmation. You can now begin tweeting.

Posting a Tweet

Start Twitter by entering **www.twitter.com** in the Address Bar of your Web browser. Sign on to Twitter with your username and password then type your message in the box under **What's happening**. The number **99** shown on the lower right below is the number of characters still available to be used out of the maximum of 140. (You don't have to use all 140 characters).

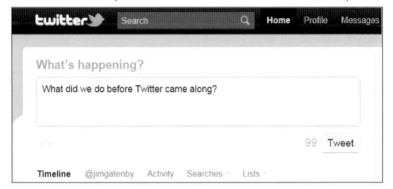

Click the **Tweet** button shown above to post the tweet.

Reading Tweets

The message is posted and is immediately available on the *timeline* or list of tweets of anyone following you, as shown below. This shows a tweet posted one minute previously by me to anyone following me. My username **@jimgatenby** is shown below. In this case the follower is Christopher Walls, username **@christowalls** — the change in spelling needed because the full name was already taken by another Twitter user.

Including an Image or Photograph with a Tweet

The icon on the right and on the lower left below allows you to add an image stored on your computer to a tweet. Click the camera icon then browse your computer and select the required image. Photos should be less than 700 kilobytes in size for posting on Twitter. A thumbnail of the image appears on the tweet as shown below. Then click the **Tweet** button to post the message.

The tweet will be available to be read by your followers almost immediately, as shown below for my follower Christopher Walls.

Twitter has embedded a link to the photograph in the tweet received by Christopher (**christowalls**). The link is the line of text **pic.twitter.com/gRT61Sk8**. (The creation of this link is done automatically for you by Twitter).

Click on the link to display the picture full size, together with the text of the tweet, as shown on the next page.

A Tweet Including a Link to a Photograph

Reducing the Size of a Photo for Posting on Twitter

As shown above, Twitter provides a very fast and easy way of sending a concise text message, together with a photograph or another sort of image. The image must be stored on your hard disc drive or removable storage device such as a flash drive or CD/DVD. As with other forms of image transfer across the Internet, very large files can cause problems, so photos should be reduced to a file size of less than 700 kilobytes. Photos can be reduced in size using programs like the freely-available Windows Live Photo Gallery or by purchasing software like the popular Adobe Photoshop Elements.

The Blog or Online Diary

The term *blog* is short for *weblog*, meaning a Web-based diary, journal or log. Like Facebook and Twitter, a blog is a form of social networking which allows people to post their thoughts onto the Internet, so that other people can read them and possibly post a comment. However, unlike Facebook, which is more about making "friends" with like-minded people, the blog is used to broadcast information about particular topics to a very wide audience. Unlike Twitter, which only allows messages of up to 140 characters, a blog can be much longer and the "blogger" can choose from a set of ready-made page design templates. Text in a blog can be formatted in different styles, images inserted and different backgrounds selected.

Many well-known radio and television journalists maintain regular blogs, reporting on the latest breaking news. Their blogs may include links to Facebook and Twitter and other Web sites. Each of these news blogs may consist of a short summary with a clickable link to a full version of the story.

The blog is really like having your own Web site, except that the page design is all taken care of for you — you don't have to know the HTML language which is used to create Web pages.

Setting up a blog is usually free and all you need to sign up and get started is a genuine e-mail address. When you set up your blog you are given a URL or Web address for the blog just like any other Web sites. After you have given the URL to your friends and relatives they can type it into the address bar of their Web browser such as Internet Explorer. So provided they know the URL for your blog, friends and relatives around the world can always see what you have to say.

A blog may contain text and images as well as links to other Web sites. As discussed on the next few pages, some blog services such as Blogger provide several ready-made design templates to choose from to give your blog a more professional look.

One of the best known programs is Blogger, created in 1999 and now owned by Google. If you log on to **www.blogger.com** you are given very simple on-screen instructions for creating your own blog. First you are asked to create a Google account by entering your e-mail address and password and agreeing to the Terms of Service. Then enter a title for the blog, as shown below.

A verification code is sent to your mobile phone as a text or voice message. This must be entered before you can continue. Since a blog is a very simple Web site you are asked to enter the Web Address or URL (Uniform Resource Locator). The address of your blog will be something like **yourname.blogspot.com** if this has not already been used. If this address is available it can be used by your friends and relatives to view your blog posts.

During the setup process you are given a choice of several Web page designs or templates on which to base your blog.

Then you're ready to start *posting* or entering the text of the blog, using the **Posting** tab in the Blogger window shown below. This has many of the features of a word-processor, including text in different styles and sizes, bold, italic, bullets, numbering and a spelling checker.

Adding a Picture to a Blog

You can insert a picture into a blog, after clicking the **Insert image** icon on the Toolbar as shown on the right and below. **Browse** to find the image on your computer then click **Add selected** to upload the picture to the blog.

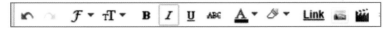

Previewing a Blog

Click the **SAVE NOW** button to save a draft of your blog. When you've finished entering the text and pictures, click **PREVIEW** to see what it will look like on the Web, as shown below.

Posting a Blog

Finally click the **PUBLISH POST** button shown on the previous page to post your blog on the Web for others to see. Other people can add comments to the blog and you can view the blogs of lots of other people. Blogs are free and can be used for any legitimate purpose, although a blog can be closed down if it is deemed offensive.

Electronic Mail

This was one of the first methods of electronic communication and remains one of the most popular and important uses of the Internet with individual users and businesses alike. Unlike the new social networking Web sites like Facebook and Twitter, it is not used to post messages for a very wide audience to see. E-mail is more like an electronic version of the traditional letter. You type a message, which can be quite lengthy and include pictures, then send it to particular people. You have to know the e-mail addresses of the people you are corresponding with, such as:

stellaaustin@hotmail.co.uk

Web-based E-mail

Some e-mail services such as Hotmail and Yahoo Mail are *Web-based*, which means all your messages are stored on the Internet on the server computers of the service provider. You can access them easily from anywhere in the world. Web-based e-mail accounts such as Hotmail are quite simple to set up.

POP 3 E-mail

E-mail services known as POP3 (Post Office Protocol) store the sent messages on their Web server computers. Next time you read your e-mail, any new messages are downloaded to your own computer. POP3 e-mail requires some setting up on a particular computer. This includes installing a program called an *e-mail client* for creating and reading messages. So it's not easy to use if you are travelling away from home, for example, and using a hotel computer. The Web-based service just requires you to get onto the Internet, type in the Web address of your mail service and sign on with your e-mail address and password.

E-mail Attachments

These are files such as reports, photos and music which can be "clipped" to an e-mail and sent with it. Web-based e-mail services may have a file size limit which requires photos, etc., to be reduced before sending, as discussed on page 200.

Creating a Hotmail Account

A Hotmail e-mail account is free to set up. Simply log on to MSN at **http://uk.msn.com**, click **Hotmail** and then click **Sign in**. If you haven't already got a Windows Live ID, click **Sign up**. You can then create your own Windows Live ID by choosing a username and password, for example, **jeansmith@live.co.uk**. This will be used as your e-mail address as well as giving access to other MSN/Windows Live services.

To sign into Windows Live, log on to **http://uk.msn.com** and select **Sign in** and enter your new e-mail address and password.

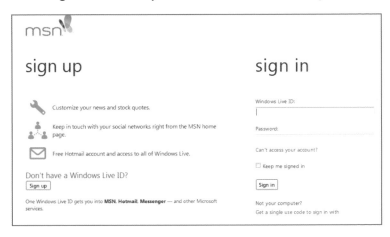

Then click **Hotmail** from the top right of the screen, followed by clicking **Inbox**, as shown below.

Receiving a Message

After signing up to Hotmail is complete, your **Inbox** receives a welcome message from the Hotmail Team, as shown below.

Click on the **Hotmail Team** entry shown above to view the full message, shown below. An e-mail can include graphics, photographs and other images, as well as links to Web sites.

As listed across the top above, there are various options to deal with a new e-mail message. After reading the message you might **Delete** it, or use **Move to** to place in a folder. As shown above there are several ready-made folders such as **Junk** and you can also create your own folders after clicking **New folder**.

If you click **Reply** shown above, a blank space opens up at the top of the message ready for you to type in your reply. The e-mail address of the original sender is automatically inserted in the **To:** slot at the top of the message. (The **To:** slot is shown on the next page.) **Reply all** sends a copy of your reply to all the recipients of the original message. Clicking **Forward** allows you to send to other people a copy of a message you have received. Type their e-mail addresses into the **To:** slot which appears and click **Send**.

Creating and Sending an E-mail

Click **New** as shown on the previous page and the following window opens. First enter the intended recipients' e-mail addresses in the **To:** bar shown below.

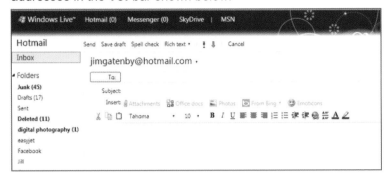

If you've e-mailed them before the addresses may be completed automatically as you type. If you want to check how your message will be received, include your own address in the list of recipients. If you click the **To:** button shown above you can select recipients from your address book or contacts list. New contacts are automatically added to your address book when they send you an e-mail. When you send an e-mail to a new contact, there is an option to add them to your address book.

Now enter a title in the **Subject:** bar. As you can see above, the e-mail program has many of the text formatting features of a word processor such as various fonts, bold, italics, coloured letters and cut and paste, etc. Start typing the new message in the blank centre panel. If you want to add files such as photos, reports, spreadsheets or pieces of music, click **Attachments** shown above. You can then browse your computer and select the required files. A link to the files is embedded in the e-mail message. Click the **Send** button to dispatch the message.

When a recipient reads their mail your message will be in their **Inbox** ready to be clicked and read. Any attachments can be opened by double-clicking the link at the top of the message.

13

Getting Creative

Introduction

This chapter looks at some of the major *applications* or programs used in the home and small business, namely:

- Word Processing
- Desktop Publishing (DTP)
- Spreadsheets (Accounts, etc.)

These applications allow you to create longer documents for printing or publication, unlike the social networking Web sites just discussed, which mainly involve short messages viewed on the screen. The above applications were in widespread use before the Internet arrived and for many years have been the backbone of most computing activity, particularly in offices.

The arrival of the Internet has revolutionised many aspects of computing and life in general; however, proficiency with the above applications remains a valuable asset for the home user who wishes to make good use of their computer. In many employment situations, knowledge of these applications is essential. They are also a major part of Computer Literacy courses such as CLAIT from the Royal Society of Arts.

These applications are provided in a suite of software known as Microsoft Office. The Home and Student Edition of Office includes the word processor Microsoft Word and the Excel spreadsheet, discussed shortly. This package costs around £70 for a single user or £85 for installation on up to 3 computers. The more expensive Office Professional contains several other programs, including the Access Database for managing records.

Word Processing and Desktop Publishing

Word processing was one of the dominant applications when micro computers were first introduced. It greatly increased office productivity because draft documents could be edited and corrected on the screen without the need for complete retyping.

Initially the word processor was used for the production of plain text without any special effects. If a document had to be formatted with special effects such as a newspaper style layout with text in columns and pictures, for example, the text from the word processor had to be imported into a separate desktop publishing program.

Nowadays the word processor has many of the features of the desktop publisher such as text in columns and the ability to include pictures and other design and page layout features. Microsoft Word is part of the Microsoft Office suite of software and is probably the most commonly used software for producing anything from a simple letter to a complete book.

For many years I have used Microsoft Word for the production of books. Word is capable of all the necessary typesetting features such as headers, footers, insertion of pictures and clip art and manipulation of text. You can also save a Word document in the popular *PDF* format (Portable Document Format) which commercial printers work from. I use the sister program Microsoft Publisher for colour books such as this one, because Publisher has specialist commercial colour printing capability (known as *CMYK*) not available in Microsoft Word. However, in other respects Microsoft Word is more than capable of the most demanding of tasks and easily satisfies the word processing and desktop publishing needs of most people..

Dedicated desktop publishing software may provide additional features for more specialist tasks such as glossy coloured leaflets, for example. For the home and small office user, Serif PagePlus and Microsoft Publisher are available for under £100.

Shown below is an extract from a 320 page book, typeset ready for the printers and produced entirely in Microsoft Word.

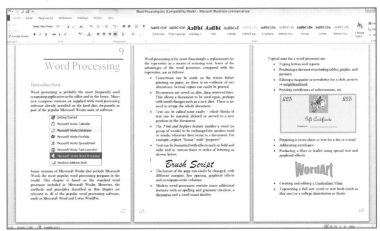

As you can see above, Microsoft Word allows you to produce documents including text in various *fonts* or styles of lettering such as **Brush Script** shown above. There are dozens of fonts to choose from after clicking the arrow to the right of the words **Times New Roman** shown below highlighted in blue.

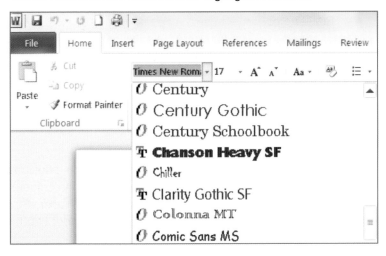

Bullets or dots are used to highlight items in a list. The extract on the previous page also shows that pictures or images such as the Gift Certificate on the right-hand page can be inserted into a document. Images can also be moved around and resized by dragging with the left-hand mouse button held down.

WordArt on the previous page is a feature in Microsoft Word and Microsoft Publisher which allows words to be manipulated and distorted into various shapes as shown below.

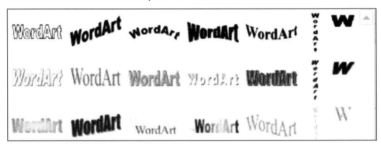

The Tabbed Ribbon

In later versions of Microsoft Office, namely Office 2007 and 2010, the traditional drop-down menus such as **File**, **Edit** and **View**, etc., have been replaced by a *tabbed ribbon* as shown below. Similar ribbons are also used in the Microsoft Excel spreadsheet and the Publisher desktop publishing program.

All of the usual tools are still available – it's just that they are presented in a different layout. There is a new **File** tab with options, for example, to **Open**, **Save** and **Print** a document, as shown on the next page.

The File Tab

When you click the **File** tab shown below, a menu appears with options to carry out major tasks such as saving and printing a document. As shown below, when you click **New**, a choice of templates is presented, providing ready-made formats and designs appropriate to the new document you wish to create.

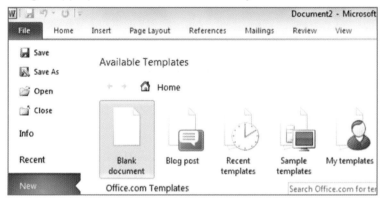

There are various other tabs on the ribbon such as **Home**, **Insert** and **Page Layout**, as shown on the previous page. Icons for related tasks are grouped together, such as the **Font** group for changing the style and size of letters. The text formatting tools such as indentation, centering, justification and line spacing are displayed in the **Paragraph** group shown on page 212.

As you change to a different task, the tools on the ribbon change automatically. For example, if you select or highlight a picture in a Word document, the **Picture Tools Format** tab appears, as shown below. Clicking this tab displays a complete set of tools for formatting a picture. An extract from the ribbon with the **Picture Tools Format** tab selected is shown below.

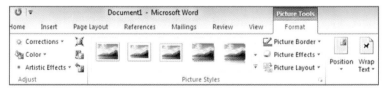

Saving a Document in Word

Save and **Save As** shown on the **File** menu on the previous page are used to make a permanent copy of your work, such as a letter about travel insurance. Clicking **Save As** opens the **Save As** dialogue box shown below.

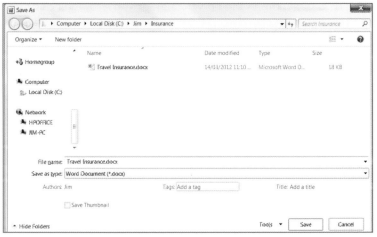

You can browse to find a folder on your computer in which to save a document, by clicking in the left-hand panel shown above. The folder may be on your hard disc drive (usually drive **C:**) or you might select a folder on a removable device like a flash drive (memory stick), usually drive **E:** or **F:**. Or you can create a new folder if you wish after clicking **New folder** shown above. In this example the document has been given the file name **Travel Insurance.docx**. The file type **.docx** is the latest Word 2010 format. If you click the arrow on the extreme right of **Save as type:**, you can save a file in the **.doc** format used by Word 97-2003. You can also save in the **.pdf** format (Portable Document Format) acceptable to most computer systems and the Internet. Click the **Save** button shown above to save the **Travel Insurance** document in the selected folder, **Insurance**, within the folder **Jim** on the **C:** drive (hard disc drive). The full path is:

C:\Jim\Insurance\Travel Insurance.docx

Word Processing and DTP Facilities

- Text can be formatted in different styles and colours.

- Text can be arranged in newspaper style columns.

- Photographs, tables, graphs and images can be inserted.

- Vast libraries of free "clip art" images are available.

- Ready-made page designs and templates can be used.

- Sentences, paragraphs and whole pages can be inserted, deleted or moved by "cutting and pasting".

- Documents can be corrected and amended on the screen without any evidence of the alterations on paper.

- *Mail merge*: Multiple copies of a standard letter infilled automatically with different names and addresses, etc.

Word Processing and DTP Tasks

- Letters, reports, newsletters, magazines, etc.

- Complete books - academic, technical, novels.

- PDF (Portable Document Format) documents — standard format suitable for sharing between computers.

- Leaflets, flyers, advertising and publicity materials.

- Business cards, greeting cards and certificates.

Word Processing and DTP Software

Professional printers and publishers may choose to use a desktop publishing program such as Adobe PageMaker, costing hundreds of pounds. Home and small business users will probably find that most of their printing and publishing needs can be accomplished using the Microsoft Word program discussed in this chapter. Serif PagePlus and Microsoft Publisher are Desktop Publishing programs aimed at the home and small business user and costing less than £100.

The Spreadsheet

Like the word processor, the spreadsheet program was one of the first applications of computers. The spreadsheet takes the hard work out of lengthy, repetitive and complex calculations. Microsoft Excel is probably the most widely used spreadsheet in the world; it is extremely powerful yet easy to learn and use. Excel is included with Microsoft Word in a suite of software known as Microsoft Office Home and Student Edition.

Microsoft Excel is a worldwide standard tool for preparing accounts in business and is also very suitable for the home user wishing to keep a tight rein on their finances. In fact the spreadsheet can be used wherever calculations are required on rows or columns of figures. Shown below is a simple spreadsheet based on plant sales in a small business.

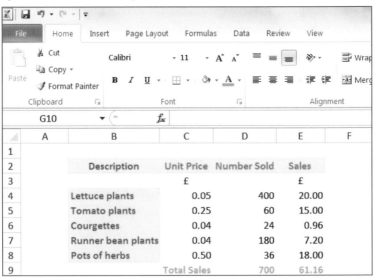

As you can see above, the spreadsheet uses a very similar tabbed ribbon to the one used in Word. This allows the spreadsheet to be formatted with different styles of text and colour. The **File** tab above is used for saving and printing.

The spreadsheet consists of a table of *cells* identified by "grid references" such as **C4** and **D4** shown below. A cell can contain text or numbers or a *formula* to carry out a calculation. Many of the formulas such as **Sum** or **Average** can be selected from the ribbon by clicking with the mouse. Others can be typed directly into a cell, preceded by an equals sign, as in **=C4*D4** shown below. (* is used for multiplication).

	A	B	C	D	E	F
1						
2		Description	Unit Price	Number Sold	Sales	
3			£		£	
4		Lettuce plants	0.05	400	=C4*D4	
5		Tomato plants	0.25	60	15.00	

Replicating a Formula

One of the great strengths of the spreadsheet is that you only have to enter a formula once at the top of a column or at the beginning of a row. Then you drag a small cross from the corner of the cell containing the formula all the way down the column or along the row. This applies the formula to all the other cells in the row or column. A big spreadsheet could have many more rows or columns than the small example shown on the previous page. This *replication* of formulas can save a great deal of work

Recalculation

Another very important facility of the spreadsheet is the ability to carry out "what if?" speculations. For example:

- What if inflation reached 7%?

- What if petrol were to cost £2.00 a litre?

- What if savings interest rates were 3%, 4%, or 5%, etc.?

The spreadsheet program makes it very easy to feed in variables like these and automatically recalculates a very large table in seconds, helping to predict possible future scenarios.

Spreadsheet Graphs and Charts

The spreadsheet program makes it easy to turn columns of figures into graphs and charts, by simply dragging over the required rows or columns and then selecting the type of graph from the Excel tabbed ribbon, shown in the extract below.

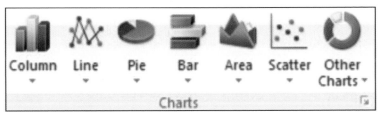

Multiple columns or rows can be selected for use in the graph by holding down the **Ctrl** key while dragging the cursor over the relevant cells with the left-hand mouse button held down. As shown in the example below, the spreadsheet program works out the scales and labels the axes automatically, tasks which are very time consuming by traditional "manual" methods.

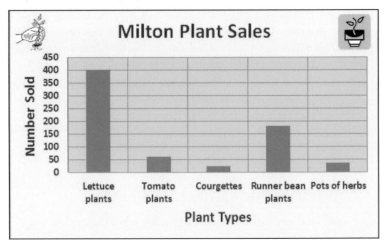

More detailed coverage of Microsoft Excel is given in our book BP701 An Introduction to Excel Spreadsheets.

14

Multimedia Activities

Introduction

The modern laptop and desktop computer can easily be used as a complete multimedia home entertainment system. The Microsoft Windows operating system installed on most computers throughout the world contains most of the software you need. Listed below are some popular multimedia activities.

- Playing music and videos from a disc in the CD/DVD drive or from files on your computer's hard disc drive.

- Downloading music and videos from the Internet, saving them on your hard disc drive or burning to a CD or DVD.

- Watching and listening to live Internet TV and radio programmes.

- Watching and listening to previously aired TV and radio programmes — "catch up" television and radio.

- Plugging a *TV tuner* dongle into your computer, to watch live Freeview television and record programmes on your computer's hard disc drive.

- Copying photographs and videos from a digital camera to your computer for viewing, editing and printing.

If you have an older machine, you might want to improve the sound quality by fitting a better quality *sound card* and some new speakers. A pair of headphones will allow you to turn up your favourite music without disturbing other people. These components can be bought quite cheaply in many computer and electrical stores and are easy to install.

The Windows Media Player

The Windows Media Player is included when Windows is first installed on your hard disc drive. It can be launched from the icon shown on the right, which is pinned as standard to the Windows Taskbar as shown below.

Playing a CD/DVD in the Windows Media Player

You can play an ordinary CD or DVD in your computer's CD/DVD drive. Simply place the disc in the drive and it should start up and play automatically.

Playing a Video Clip Stored on the Computer

The following video clip was taken with a compact digital camera and transferred to the hard disc drive as described shortly. The video clip is the icon on the left shown below in the Windows Explorer. (**.MOV** is the movie file format for the QuickTime player from Apple. **.MOV** files can also be played in the Windows Media Player.) The file on the right below is a still photo with the normal **.JPG** or **JPEG** extension (Joint Photographic Experts Group.)

Double-clicking the name or icon for the video in the Windows Explorer opens the video in the Windows Media Player, as shown on the next page.

The Windows Media Player has the usual media player controls as shown enlarged below.

Reading from the left, there are icons to turn **Shuffle** and **Repeat** on, followed by **Stop** and **Rewind**. In the centre is the **Play/Pause** button followed by **Fast Forward**, **Mute** and the **Volume** control slider.

In the bottom right-hand corner of the Windows Media Player screen above is an icon (shown here on the right) which switches between **View full screen** or **Exit full screen**. In the top right-hand corner is an icon (shown here on the right) to switch to the Windows Media Player Library, (discussed shortly).

The Media Player Library

As discussed previously, the Windows Media Player is launched automatically when you insert a CD or DVD. However, you will probably build up a library of your own music and videos, stored on your computer's internal hard disc, as discussed shortly. The Windows Media Player can be opened by clicking its icon on the Windows Taskbar, as shown on the right and below.

The **Library** opens as shown below, with a number of categories down the left-hand side.

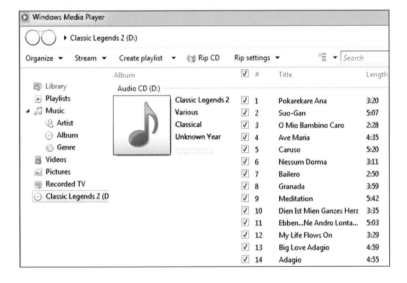

Music can be organized and displayed in various categories i.e. **Artist**, **Album** and **Genre**.

Playlists are collections of favourite tracks created by the user by dragging music tracks onto the **Play** tab on the right of the Windows Media Player, as shown on page 225.

Copying Music from a CD to Your Hard Disc

If you buy a music CD it's very convenient to copy it onto your computer. Then you can create playlists of your favourite tracks which can be played in the background while you are working on the computer.

When there is a music CD in the drive, all of the tracks on the CD are listed in the Windows Media Player, as shown on the previous page. Initially all of the tracks are selected with a tick; any track which you don't want to copy can be excluded by clicking the adjacent check box to remove the tick.
Now click **Rip CD** as shown on the right and on the
previous page to start the copying process. You
are informed of progress as the ticks are steadily removed to indicate that the tracks have been copied to the **Library**.

The newly copied music on the hard disc, **Let's Get Classical** in this example, can then be displayed in the **Library**, in one of the categories, such as **Album** for example, shown below.

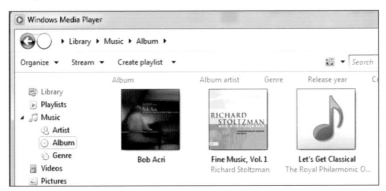

To play one of the tracks, double-click the album, then select the track and click the **Play** icon shown on the right and below. Or simply double-click the track.

Downloading Music from the Internet

Many online stores such as Amazon sell music to be downloaded straight to your computer's hard disc drive. For example, log on to Amazon by entering their address in your Web browser:

www.amazon.co.uk

MP3 is a common format for downloading music files and Amazon provides a button to download the **Amazon MP3 Downloader** to speed up the process. After browsing through the categories to find the music you want you can view the prices and play some short samples of the tracks.

Any tracks or albums can be added to your shopping basket. If you've already signed up for an account with Amazon giving all your address and bank details, the entire transaction can be completed by clicking the **1-click** button shown on the next page. Otherwise sign up for an account and complete the purchase.

After completing the purchase, click the download button and the tracks or albums are downloaded to the **My Music** folder in your **Music Library** on your hard disc drive, as shown below

Double-click a track to play it in the Windows Media Player. Or open the Media Player by clicking its icon (shown right) on the Taskbar. Then select the track and click the **Play** button.

Burning Music to a CD

You can burn music to a CD by selecting the **Burn** tab on the right of the Media Player. Then drag the required tracks to the space under **Burn list**. When you insert a blank CD, the burning process should start, otherwise click **Start burn**.

Live and Catch Up Television

Some of the major television and radio channels can now be received live on your computer. All you need is an Internet connection and some software such as *BBC iPlayer*. This software is free and can be downloaded from :

www.bbc.co.uk/iplayer/install

With iPlayer you can also watch recordings of the last 7 days' programmes. *ITV Player* is a free Web site which also allows you to watch "catch up" television, i.e. programmes broadcast previously. You can start using the ITV Player Web site at:

www.itv.com/itvplayer

Downloading

BBC iPlayer allows you to *download* a TV programme from the Internet to your computer and save it on your hard disc drive.

The Windows Media Center

As discussed on the previous page, some TV and radio channels can be viewed via the Internet with no special equipment other than an Internet connection.

However, to receive the full range of over 100 Freeview digital television and radio channels you need to obtain a *TV Tuner*. This can take the form of a *dongle*, which plugs into one of the small  rectangular USB ports on the computer. The other end of the tuner connects to a TV aerial; the aerial may be part of a TV Tuner kit. However, in some locations you may get better results by connecting the tuner to a normal domestic TV aerial. Tuner kits typically cost £15 — £70.

Your computer already contains everything else needed to watch television, including the Windows Media Center software. The hard disc is used to record programs and the normal speakers and monitor provide the sound and vision. Once set up, the Media Center computer allows you to:

- Watch live digital television and radio.

- Pause, instantly replay then continue live TV programmes.

- Use your hard disc to record and replay programmes quickly and easily.

- Use a 14-day programme guide to schedule recordings in advance.

- Easily delete programmes from the hard disc.

- Burn TV programmes to DVD disc in the standard MPEG-2 video format used in DVD players.

The **settings** menu in the Windows Media Center requires you to enter your UK region and postcode. From this information a choice of local transmitters is provided and a **TV Guide** listing TV and radio programs for the next 14 days is downloaded.

When the TV Guide is complete, the Windows Media Center starts scanning for channels. After finding all the available channels you can enjoy the whole range of Freeview TV programs and various radio channels shown in the extract below. Channels can be selected by using a mouse and the on-screen control bar shown on the right below. Alternatively a TV remote control can be used to operate the television; this is usually supplied as part of the TV tuner kit.

Digital Photography on Your Computer

Your computer can be used to store, manage, edit and share your digital photographs. A program called Windows Live Photo Gallery provides all of the necessary facilities and can be downloaded free from the following Microsoft Web site:

http://explore.live.com

Copying Photos from a Digital Camera

A cable is often used to connect the camera to one of the small rectangular USB ports on the computer. Alternatively some computers and printers have a slot which accepts a camera's memory card. The computer detects the camera or memory card as **Removable Disk (E:)** or **(F:)**, etc., as shown on the right in the **AutoPlay** window which pops up.

Click **Import pictures and videos using Windows Live Photo Gallery** and then select with a tick the pictures you want to import or just click **Select all**.

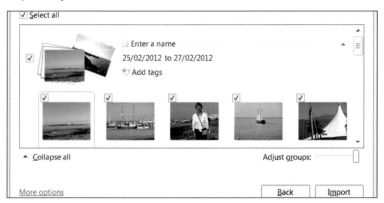

After selecting the photos and clicking the **Import** button, the images are copied to the Windows Live Photo Gallery on your computer's hard disc drive, which opens as shown below.

Double-click any of the thumbnail images shown above and the photograph opens on the full screen as shown below, ready for you to carry out a wide   range of editing tasks. These include cropping the image, removing "red eye", adjusting the colours, the brightness and contrast and straightening and rotating, etc.

After editing, an image can be saved as a .jpg (JPEG) file, printed on paper, viewed in a slide show, e-mailed or posted to a Web site such as Facebook, Twitter, Flickr or YouTube.

You can create a secure archive of your photos using the option **Burn a CD** on the Windows Live Photo Gallery **File** menu.

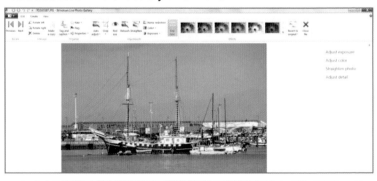

More detailed coverage of this subject given in our book BP729 Computing and Digital Photography for the Older Generation from Bernard Babani (publishing) Ltd.

Useful Software Tools

This chapter looks at some of the utility programs available to manage your computer and keep it working properly. Most of these are installed on your hard disc as part of the Windows operating system or alternatively they can be freely downloaded.

Windows Easy Transfer

This program is used to simplify the task of copying your essential files from one computer to another. For example, you buy a new Windows 7 computer and want to copy to the new machine all of your documents, e-mails, videos and photos, etc., from an older machine running Windows XP or Vista.

Easy Transfer copies your personal files, not programs, to the new machine. Programs have to be installed from their original CDs or by downloading from the Internet.

Easy Transfer has to be installed on both computers. It is automatically installed as part of Windows 7 and users of other versions of Windows can download a free copy from:

www.microsoft.com/download

There are three physical methods of making the transfer:

- Connecting the two machines using a special Easy Transfer USB cable, available from computer stores. This package includes software for the cable on a CD.

- Transferring files across a network to which both computers are connected.

- Copying all of the files to a single Easy Transfer file on an external hard disc drive. For a smaller quantity of data a removable USB flash drive may be adequate.

In this section "old" and "new" refer to the source and destination computers, although Easy Transfer can also be used when a single computer is being upgraded, say, from Windows XP to Windows 7. In this case an external hard disc would be used.

It is recommended that you start by running Easy Transfer on the new machine. If using an Easy Transfer cable, don't connect it until instructed. On Windows 7 the program can be launched by clicking the **Start** button and entering **Easy Transfer** in the *Search programs and files* bar at the bottom left of the screen. First you are asked to select the method to be used — Easy Transfer cable, network or external hard drive/flash drive as mentioned above. The next part of the procedure depends on which of the three transfer methods is selected. As usual, with all of these step-by-step processes, it is a case of following the instructions and responding to questions on the screen before clicking the **Next** button to continue.

If necessary you are given an option to copy the Easy Transfer program to a flash drive and then guided through the process of installing it on the old machine. When Easy Transfer is running on both machines you are asked to connect them using the Easy Transfer cable or alternatively plug in the external hard disc drive or flash drive on the old machine. If using an external hard disc drive or flash drive a single Easy Transfer File is created and this contains all the files in the transfer. You are told to browse to the location where the Easy Transfer File is to be saved.

If you are using Easy Transfer across a network you are asked to start the program on the new machine first. Then, when instructed, start Easy Transfer on the old machine and note the *Easy Transfer key* which is generated. This is then entered in the new machine to complete the Easy Transfer network connection.

> Windows Easy Transfer key:
>
> **545-696**

With the two machines connected and running Easy Transfer, or with the old machine connected to the external hard disc drive or flash drive, the old computer is scanned. A default selection of files to be transferred is displayed by Easy Transfer. You can modify this list of files after clicking **Customize**, as shown below.

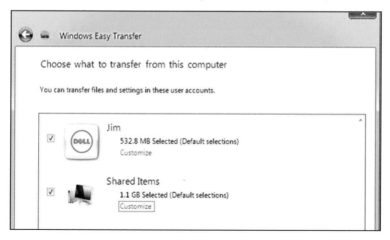

After you click **Next** the files are transferred directly to the new computer or to the external hard disc drive or flash drive.

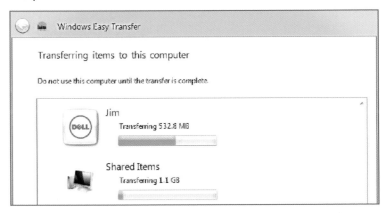

Using the external hard disc drive or flash drive, a single Easy Transfer File is saved on the drive and a password can be added. You are advised to write down the location of the transfer file so you can open it in Easy Transfer on the new machine. When the transfer is complete you can display a list of the files transferred and their locations on the new machine, such as **C:\Users\Jim\Pictures**. There is also an option to display a list of programs on your old machine that you might wish to install on the new computer. (Programs must be installed from the original CDs/DVDs or by downloading, not by Easy Transfer.)

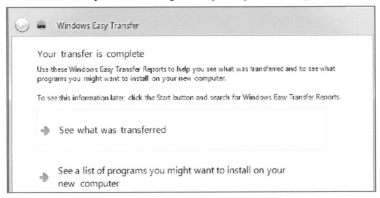

Windows Backup

Easy Transfer just described is intended to migrate all of your personal files from an old computer to a new one. Whereas the purpose of Windows Backup is to make duplicate copies of important files for security, on a separate medium such as a flash drive, CD/DVD or external hard disc drive. Then if the original files are lost or damaged, the backup copies can be restored.

Click **Start**, **Control Panel** and under **System and Security** select **Back up your computer**. Then click **Set up backup** and choose where you want to store the backup files. For a large backup an external hard disc drive is recommended. After clicking **Next**, you can then choose the files you want to back up.

You can allow Windows to decide what to back up or click **Let me choose** and select the required folders and files to back up in the Windows Explorer as shown below.

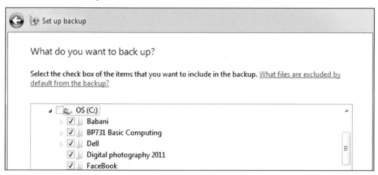

For a few files or folders you can probably use a flash drive. A large backup requires an external hard disc drive and a *disc image* may be saved on the external hard disc drive. A disc image is a copy of the whole hard disc in a single file. Separate files and folders cannot be extracted from a disc image.

After clicking **Next** you can **Revue your backup settings** before clicking **Save settings and run backup** as shown on the next page. You can also change the time for a scheduled backup.

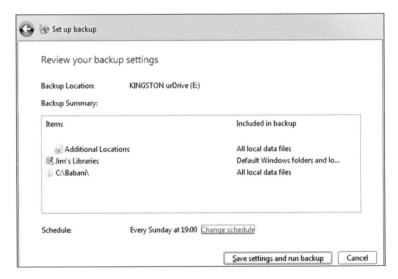

The **Backup and Restore** window opens as shown below, giving progress of the backup. At a later date, if necessary, files and folders from the backup can be restored after clicking the **Restore my files** button shown at the bottom right below. You can restore all of the files or just a selection, to the original location or to a new location, on another computer if necessary.

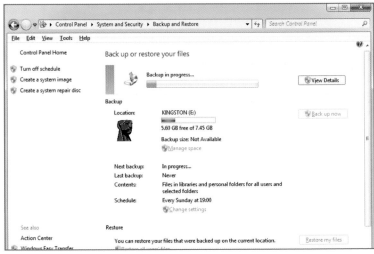

Windows System Tools

Microsoft Windows includes a number of utilities to keep your computer running efficiently. These can be displayed by clicking **Start**, **All Programs**, **Accessories** and **System Tools**, as shown in the small extract on the right.

Disk Cleanup

During normal running, your computer saves a lot of temporary files on the hard disc drive. For example, copies of Web pages are saved to make them quicker to open during future Web browsing sessions. Also files you "delete" are sent to a folder called the **Recycle Bin**. They are not actually removed from the hard disc until the **Recycle Bin** is emptied. If you have too many redundant files cluttering up your hard disc, the computer might run slowly. Clicking **Disk Cleanup** shown above calculates how much space can be saved and allows you to delete redundant files and empty the **Recycle Bin**.

Disk Defragmenter

After a period of time, parts of files on a hard disc become scattered after all the saving, deleting and changing. This slows down the process of finding and opening a file since the latest changes to a file may be in different locations from the original file. If you click **Disk Defragmenter** shown above, and select the hard disc, it is analysed and if necessary the files are rearranged or consolidated to make the computer run more efficiently. **Disk Defragmenter** should be run regularly and can be scheduled for a specific time each week, as shown below. You can also carry out a manual defragmentation at any time.

System Restore

Sometimes when you install a new piece of software or hardware, the computer may stop working properly. **System Restore**, shown on the **Systems Tools** menu on the previous page, returns the computer's critical settings to a previous time when it was working correctly. **Restore Points** are "snapshots" taken at regular intervals of all the important settings. (**System Restore** doesn't make copies of your work or data files, which should be backed up regularly as discussed earlier.) **Restore Points** can also be created manually before major changes.

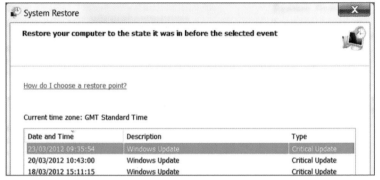

Windows Update

This feature downloads to your computer the latest modifications and upgrades to the Microsoft Windows operating system. Click **Start**, **All Programs**, **Windows Update, Change settings** and make sure **Install updates automatically** is turned on.

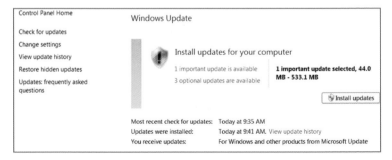

Windows Security

The Internet provides enormous opportunities in many walks of life — work, education, entertainment, communicating with friends and family, etc., etc. However, such powerful technology also brings with it the potential for illegal and antisocial activities. These include the spreading of *malware* (malicious software) such as *viruses*, *worms* and *Trojan horses*. Malware may be spread by the Internet, for example in an attachment to an e-mail message. Malware is intended to damage your files or spoil the performance of your computer. *Spyware* covertly tries to find out personal and financial information, such as bank details, Web browsing activities and it may even monitor your keystrokes.

You can check the security status of your computer after clicking the small flag on the Notification Area on the right of the Taskbar at the bottom of the screen. Then click **Open Action Center** from the bottom of the pop-up window. Finally click the downward arrow on the right of **Security** to see your computer's security settings, as shown below.

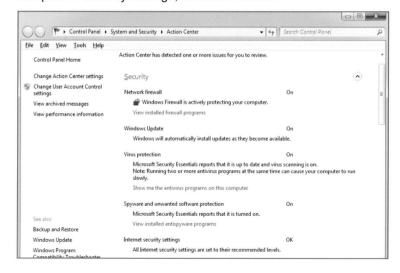

The **Action Center** shown on the previous page reports the status of the security software on your computer.

The *Windows Firewall* is intended to stop unwanted Internet "traffic", (malware, etc.), entering or leaving your computer. The Windows Firewall is included in Windows 7, XP and Vista.

Windows Defender scans your computer for any spyware monitoring your activities. The Defender is included in Windows 7 and Vista and available as a free download for XP from **www.microsoft.com/download**. The Windows Firewall and Windows Defender can be switched on or off after clicking their icons in the **Control Panel**, shown below in **Large icons** view.

Windows does not include its own antivirus software but *Microsoft Security Essentials* is available as a free download from **www.microsoft.com/download**. This provides antivirus and antispyware scanning and protection, as shown below.

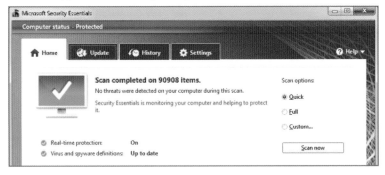

Alternatively you could install third party security and antivirus software, such as Norton Internet Security or Kaspersky Internet Security. Your computer should detect this software and report its status in the Action Center, as shown on the previous page. You should not have more than one antivirus or Internet security program installed as this may spoil your computer's performance.

Notes for Users of Windows XP

This book was produced using a PC computer running the Windows 7 operating system. However, many people are still using earlier versions of Windows such as XP and Vista. The material in this book should be completely compatible with machines running Windows Vista. The general methods in this book are also broadly compatible with Windows XP, although there are some slight differences. The XP user interface is very similar, with icons for programs on the Windows Desktop and the Taskbar along the bottom showing running programs.

There are some cosmetic differences in the screen designs. For example, Windows XP uses the rectangular **Start** button shown on the right, while Windows 7 uses a round button. In Windows XP **My Computer** is launched from the **Start** menu while in Windows 7 there is the **Windows Explorer** icon shown on the right, permanently pinned to the Taskbar. **My Computer** in Windows XP uses menus in the left-hand panel as shown below while the **Computer** feature in Windows 7 displays folders and libraries.

The Tabbed Ribbon vs File, Edit and View, etc.

Later Microsoft Office and Paint programs display the Tabbed Ribbon across the top of the screen, rather than the **File**, **Edit**, **View**… Menu Bar previously used and shown below.

Later versions of programs like Microsoft Word and Excel, which use Tabbed Ribbons, as described in this book, can also be used with Windows XP.

Internet Explorer

Windows XP can run the Internet Explorer Web browser, so users of XP can make full use of programs and Web sites such as Google, Hotmail, Facebook, Twitter and Skype. Windows XP has its own built-in e-mail client, known as Outlook Express. Users of Windows 7 need to download an e-mail *client* program, Windows Live Mail, if they want to store e-mails on their computer's hard disc drive like users of XP and Outlook Express.

Windows Live Photo Gallery for Windows XP

A free download can be made from **http://explore.live.com**.

Utility Software

Most of the Windows utility features covered in this book are also available in Windows XP, such as the **Control Panel**, **System Tools**, **Disk Cleanup**, **Disk Defragmenter** and **System Restore**. These are available from **Start**, **All Programs**, **Accessories** and **System Tools**. Special needs features, known as **Ease of Access** in Windows 7, can be found in Windows XP at **Start**, **All Programs** and **Accessibility**. **Easy Transfer** for Windows XP is obtainable as described on pages 232 and 233.

In Windows XP, the **Windows Firewall** can be switched on after clicking **Start**, **Control Panel** and double-clicking its icon, as shown on the right.

Windows
Firewall

Index